ENDORSEMENTS

The level of teaching that Pastor Gary Whetstone brings to the table is absolutely incredible! You need this. It's going to take you to the next level. When you get an opportunity to hear something that Pastor Whetstone has endorsed and prepared, you are hearing from somebody who's not just been in the boardroom, but has been right there on the field fighting—and he knows what he's talking about.

—*Bishop T.D. Jakes*
The Potter's House
Dallas, Texas

There could be no more suitable subject for these perilous times, and no one in his lifetime is exempt. The need is universal, and the solution is spiritual. In this book, Gary Whetstone provides us with many succinct and viable answers that can only free and strengthen.

—*Charles E. Blair*
Pastor Emeritus, Calvary Temple
Denver, Colorado

It gives me a great deal of personal and spiritual satisfaction to share a few words on Brother Whetstone's new book, *Make Fear Bow.*

I have known Gary Whetstone for over twelve years. We have traveled together throughout the nations of the world. It has been my joy to see firsthand the mighty anointing of God upon Gary as he teaches God's Word to countless multitudes.

Make Fear Bow is destined to flow in this same anointing—a balanced teaching of God's holy Word.

When you apply the truths outlined in this book, any fears you may have possessed will be destroyed because of the anointing!

—*Morris Cerullo*
President, Morris Cerullo World Evangelism
San Diego, California

I believe all those who come under the anointed teaching and the ministry of Pastor Whetstone will be thoroughly equipped to gather in the end-time harvest before the imminent return of our Lord and Savior Jesus Christ.

—*Rod Parsley*
Senior Pastor, World Harvest Church
Columbus, Ohio

MAKE Fear BOW

GARY V. WHETSTONE

WHITAKER
HOUSE

MAKE FEAR BOW

Gary Whetstone Worldwide Ministries
P. O. Box 10050
Wilmington, DE 19850
www.gwwm.com
Email: info@gwwm.com

ISBN: 978-0-88368-776-5
eBook ISBN: 978-1-60374-855-1
Printed in the United States of America
© 2002 by Gary V. Whetstone

Whitaker House
1030 Hunt Valley Circle
New Kensington, PA 15068
www.whitakerhouse.com

Library of Congress Cataloging-in-Publication Control Number: 2002008245

2 3 4 5 6 7 8 9 10 11   ᵾ   19 18 17 16 15 14 13

CONTENTS

Does a perimeter of fear keep you within its limiting boundary? Are you stuck in a repetitive cycle of failure? Do you want God's anointing to lift the weight of oppression from you and break the yoke that has held you back? Then you are ready for your appointment with freedom!

Understanding what fear is and where it comes from can set you free from its paralyzing grip. Then you can pursue the dreams God has planned for you. Jesus has already paid the price for your freedom from fear. Don't allow fear to paralyze you. Instead, make fear bow, in Jesus' name!

One of the major causes of fear is relying on what the Bible calls the *"arm of flesh"* (2 Chronicles 32:8). That's when we focus on and trust in our own abilities to cope or deal with problems. Are you questioning whether you should go forward because of so many challenges? Are you afraid you cannot overcome them? God is with you, ready to help you accomplish your dreams!

Many people become weighed down by fear as a result of how their circumstances appear. Constantly feeding on this type of information without applying God's Good News can have a devastating impact. God has miracles planned for you, but you must trust and obey Him despite the apparent circumstances.

If we do not know how to silence our powerful negative reactions, runaway emotions can control our lives. Are you continually affected negatively by what you see, hear, smell, taste, or feel? Is your life riddled with tension? Our senses can limit us and bring us into great bondage, but God wants to enlarge our borders and deliver us from a spirit of fear!

FOREWORD

Gary Whetstone has written the most complete book I've ever read on fear—where it comes from and how to get rid of it.

It not only deals with every kind of fear and all the ways fear can sneak in, it also shows how to positively overcome it in every area of life. I love Gary's acrostic for fear:

F—False

E—Evidence

A—Appearing

R—Real

You'll discover that fear's false imagery creates torment that exists in the imagination—but is all too real. You also may find that "calculated pessimism," an insidious deception, is making your life "smaller" than it ought to be.

Gary's book shows how you can break free from the fear-crippled masses of "not able" people to join the fear-less ones who are empowered and able to do *"all things through Christ"* (Philippians 4:13). There is no question, this book is a must read for every Christian!

When you read *Make Fear Bow,* the devil and his deceptions will be revealed. He will have to flee—and you will be set free! You really can escape—live fear-free—and this book will show you how.

—*Marilyn Hickey*
Marilyn Hickey Ministries

"Fear not, for I am with you; be not dismayed, for I am your God.
I will strengthen you, Yes, I will help you,
I will uphold you with My righteous right hand."
—Isaiah 41:10

"For God has not given us a spirit of fear,
but of power and of love and of a sound mind."
—2 Timothy 1:7

CHAPTER ONE

HOW TO TRAIN AN ELEPHANT

I didn't mean to startle you," apologized the young man. He had accidentally bumped into Anne as she came out of her hotel room in Chicago.

In a flash, the middle-aged woman recalled the trauma that her younger sister had experienced five years earlier—she had been raped at knifepoint! Afraid that the same thing would happen to her, Anne allowed a harmless encounter to catapult her into a whirlwind of fear.

She could not call home to tell her husband. They had just agreed that she could travel alone again. She could not confide in her boss. The last thing he wanted to hear was that his employee was too fearful to get the job done. Her sister was not an option, either. So, one more time, Anne stuffed her hidden fears deeper within herself. *After all, who can really help me?* she wondered as another restless night dragged on.

For more of us than we want to admit, fear is a debilitating force. It freezes us in its grip, like a cold hand muzzling our mouths. Trapped by it, we can't scream, and we can't get free.

Beth will never forget how a relative sexually molested her. The first time, she was only a small child; then it happened again when she was a teenager.

11

Without realizing it, she developed a fear of men. When Beth went away to college, she met Todd, who, throughout their college years, clearly demonstrated that not *all* men would hurt her. He loved her from the start, and he proved himself to her over the years. His tenderness and gentleness broke down Beth's defenses, and she began to love and trust him.

One day, Todd proposed to her. Beth was thrilled and wanted to marry him, but fear gripped her. She seriously considered not marrying the man she loved because, although she trusted him, she did not know if she could handle the physical intimacy of marriage.

Living in Fear

Are you locked in fear's immobilizing grip?

Does fear have you in its grip? How much time do you spend worrying, suspecting, dreading, doubting, questioning, or expecting the worst? Are you cowering from the life God has intended for you because you are afraid to step out in faith? Have the images in your mind already painted you into failure's dead-end? Do you often feel threatened or restless? Do you live in the torment of constant fear, daily struggling to find a solution to the disaster you imagine is looming ahead?

Maybe you've just watched a television show that portrayed a vicious crime; now, you fear for the safety of your family. In the middle of the night, when the wind gently blows the curtains, is your mind locked in a vise of fear that a drug-crazed gang member or burglar has entered your house? If you hear sirens, are you convinced that a family member has been in a terrible accident? Do you fear contracting HIV or AIDS when you find yourself shaking hands with a frail man who looks sick? Fear can grip you, immobilizing you, or it can cause you to jump to extreme conclusions.

Chuck still recalls from his childhood what happened every time he sat down to eat fish for dinner with his family. Throughout the meal, he would hear the story repeatedly told of how his Uncle Bob had choked to death on a fish bone. First, his uncle couldn't breathe. Then he grabbed his neck, turned blue, and beckoned for help as everyone helplessly watched him die at the table. Chuck cannot forget the tension he sensed as a child at dinnertime. If he coughed, the adults panicked. Immediately, someone would slap his back vigorously, and another would shove a glass of water in his direction. The same story still plays out in Chuck's mind today. For years, he refused to eat fish because of the fear-encoded message ingrained in him: "Small bones can kill you—just like they did your Uncle Bob!"

Fears Develop in Many Forms

Fears, which manifest themselves in many different ways, plague people every day. Some people have phobias about flying. Others fear driving. Some become terribly nervous when, instead of driving themselves, they take the passenger's seat. Some are afraid to ride in elevators, while others are fearful of crossing streets. The fear of water or going across bridges enslaves still others.

Many, who are single from divorce, are terrified of ever remarrying again. Others, who have never been married, are afraid of making the wrong choice for a mate. Some married couples are afraid of staying married, while others fear divorce will strike them.

Some people fear darkness, small places, or heights. Many fear going to their doctors—afraid they will hear some dreaded diagnosis. Others seek medical attention continually, even though their complaints are nothing more than psychosomatic.

Some fear going out to public places, such as to shopping malls, athletic events, or even to the grocery store. Others are afraid of staying home and interacting with their spouses and family members. Some men crash in the area of communication because the fear of human relationships binds them. Fear cripples and destroys some married women who are afraid that, if they gain weight, their husbands will no longer find them desirable.

Your Appointment with Freedom

You do not need to be bound by your fears! Today, you are holding in your hands an appointment with freedom. Unfortunately, many of the people you know will never experience the freedom that is theirs, but *you* can change that! Yes, *your* freedom can liberate not only you but also those around you.

This book, *Make Fear Bow*, has come to me as a mandate from Jesus. It happened during the month of September, as summer drew to a close. I was in a time of prayer when the Spirit of the Lord spoke to me. He instructed me to take the more than two thousand prayer requests that had come into our ministry during that one week, fly to London, and stay in a hotel room to pray for them. I was also to stand in support of a major spiritual breakthrough for the United Kingdom and Europe.

> Your freedom can be the means of liberating someone else.

As I spent hour upon hour in prayer over the requests, I began to notice something extremely alarming that grieved my spirit. More than 80 percent of all the written prayer requests had one common element: fear! I read about the fear of marriage failure; fear of children leaving home; fear of being unable to cope with retirement; fear of being in elevators; fear of taking tests; fear of greeting new people; fears that, in the middle of the night, creep from the imaginations of the mind; and many others too numerous to list. These fears became so evident among the prayer requests that by the second day of my time of prayer, I went back through them with a red pen and marked every one that had fear as its underlying cause. Then I categorized them from family concerns to personal inadequacies to senses of timidity to absolute paralysis and inability to cope with life.

Today, as you begin to read, I want you to understand my heart and the reason for this book. It is simply because the Holy Spirit has targeted one of the major strongholds that has affected the body of Christ. Intimidation and bondage have infected every aspect and walk of life, and the result is devastating. This stronghold has greatly diminished and almost neutered the effectiveness of the Christian life. But God can change all that!

During the week of prayer in England, I met with people from several major international ministries and explained what had been happening in my prayer time. In Earl's Court of London, England, we launched a prayer ministry that yielded breakthrough after breakthrough. Literally, within one day, we broke major strongholds that had held back the church that Jesus purchased by His own blood. Throughout that week, we violently waged war against fear through prayer.

The greatest fear gripping the ministers there was breaking the hold that traditions had on them. When their fears were exposed, we were able to destroy the façade that had been created by their religious rituals. Now, the devil was in trouble.

It was time to turn on the light and drive fear from their lives. They had been bound by the fear and shame brought about by preaching a message of freedom while still being captives themselves. As they became open, candid, and repentant, they were set free to experience and live in the liberty of Christ that they had been preaching about!

I had struck the devil's nerve center! Throughout this book, we will hit him over and over again until *you step into the liberation God has promised to you!*

God gave me explicit instructions to research the Word of God and uncover every cause and the resultant effects of fear. What I discovered is one of the most powerful revelations I have ever shared. Today, this message continues to transform lives.

Break the Tie that Binds

One of the prayer requests I took to London was from a single woman in her mid-twenties. She wrote that, years before, she had become pregnant before marriage and had never finished high school. Now, she had two children. When the young woman reflected upon her life, her mother's constant negative statements repeatedly sounded in her ears.

Her mother also had children out of wedlock and had never graduated from high school. Constantly, she nagged her daughter, saying things like, "You'll never make anything of your life. You'll be just like me. You'll constantly go from man to man. No one will ever want you. Nobody will love you. You'll be happy if someone will just give you the time of day. You're used goods…that's all…used goods!" *Yes, that sums up my life—used goods,* the young woman thought.

When I received this single mother's prayer request, she feared that what her mother had spoken over her life would become her reality. Then she heard my teaching on *Make Fear Bow.* After setting her life right with God, she determined that her mother's words would *not* rule her life. This young woman conquered those fears and, as a result, now has a very strong self-image. She has a successful job, and her children are doing well. Her life will never be the same!

Do you see how that mother's words bound this young woman in fear? Those words became a rope that tied the mother's past to her daughter's future. They doomed the young woman to the fears of failure, loneliness, and never finding love or happiness. As a result, inadequacy, shame, and guilt continually tormented her. Finally, when she heard the truth about her fears, it set her free. She broke that tie that had bound her for her entire life. That is how powerful this message of *Make Fear Bow* is! However, unless you know you are bound, you will not seek to be set free.

> What is your limiting factor?

Let me explain. Do you know how to train an elephant? When a baby elephant is born, it knows only one thing: Mom! She is her baby's primary place of safety and source of nourishment. As long as the mother is tied with a length of rope to the stake, the baby elephant stays within the limits of the mother out of necessity.

Soon the baby elephant's leg is tied to its own rope and stake. The rope is not very thick and is not driven very deeply into the ground. Early on, the baby elephant knows its limitations. It can go only as far as the rope will allow.

Several years later, when the baby has grown, the animal is an ominous sight. Although it possesses immense strength, its leg is still tied to a thin rope. The length of the rope from the post is the only distance this huge, powerful animal will go. Anyone can see that with only a slight effort, the elephant could snap the rope in two. Yet it does not! Why?

Tied to the stake, that rope has always been the elephant's limiting factor in life. Years later, when the elephant feels the slightest resistance from the rope, although the animal is thousands of pounds heavier, it believes that it can go no farther.

This illustrates the power of a yoke. Today, many people are bound to the limits of a repetitive cycle of attitude, frustration, fear, behavior, and other bondages. Although the "Greater One" lives within them, they accept these false limits as the boundaries of their lives.

Have you been trained like an elephant? Does the old perimeter of fear still stand as your limiting boundary? As you read this book, open your heart wide. Let the revelation of God's insights and wisdom unfold within you. He will reveal your true spiritual nature and purpose. Allow the anointing of God to lift the weight of oppression from you and break the yoke that fear has caused. Accept God's promise for you:

And it shall come to pass in that day, that his burden shall be taken away from off thy shoulder, and his yoke from off thy neck, and the yoke shall be destroyed because of the anointing. (Isaiah 10:27 KJV)

Let's get hooked up together with God to break the yokes that bind your life!

CHAPTER TWO

THE ORIGIN OF FEAR

When fear enslaves people, a devastating, crippling force holds them at bay. Although they have significant dreams, when it comes to implementing them, they stop dead in their tracks. Instead of proceeding forward, they have a multitude of excuses why they cannot accomplish their visions. But no legitimate reasons are holding them back; it is their fear!

God wants to remove that fear, though, and turn their lives into exciting adventures. Then they will be filled with His love and peace and experience great fulfillment. Nothing will be able to hold them back from the exploits of faith that God desires for them to do.

In order to confront fear, we must understand what it is and where it originated. These revelations can set us free from fear's paralyzing grip so that we can pursue the dreams God has planned for us. Jesus already paid the price for our freedom from fear. Are you ready to walk in that freedom?

The Entrance of Fear

After God created Adam, He put man in the garden of Eden, which He had planted. Here we see God as a loving, nurturing Father.

The LORD God planted a garden eastward in Eden, and there He put the man whom He had formed. And out of the ground the LORD God made every tree grow that is pleasant to the sight and good for food. The tree of life was also in the midst of the garden, and the tree of the knowledge of good and evil. (Genesis 2:8–9)

What was in the garden of Eden with man? Notice, there were three types of trees:

+ One type was pleasant to see and bore fruit for food.
+ The second was the Tree of Life.
+ The third was the Tree of Knowledge of Good and Evil.

God issued an important instruction to Adam about this third tree:

And the LORD God commanded the man, saying, "Of every tree of the garden you may freely eat; but of the tree of the knowledge of good and evil you shall not eat, for in the day that you eat of it you shall surely die." (verses 16–17)

It is critical to understand that the fruits of this third tree are not apples or other similar physical fruits, as many artists have depicted. Remember, this is the Tree of Knowledge. Therefore, its fruit is knowledge. "Eating" from the Tree of Knowledge of Good and Evil means partaking of a new kind of knowledge. This knowledge allows one to understand good and evil, not merely good as God had originally created man to know. Therefore, partaking of the Tree of Knowledge of Good and Evil means receiving information from a new source other than God. This evil source is Satan.

God warned Adam that ingesting this new knowledge would result in eternal death in place of the eternal life he was then enjoying.

Satan, in the form of a serpent, tempted Adam's wife, Eve. As a result, Adam and Eve disobeyed God and ate of this third tree's forbidden fruit. Consequently, as Genesis explains, their eyes became opened to see good and evil:

For God knows that when you eat of it your eyes will be opened, and you will be like God, knowing good and evil. (Genesis 3:5 NIV)

*And the L*ORD *God said, "The man has now become like one of us, knowing good and evil."* (Genesis 3:22 NIV)

What were the effects of ingesting this new knowledge? One of the first signs of eating from the Tree of Knowledge of Good and Evil was fear. Observe Adam's and Eve's responses after they ate:

*And they heard the sound of the L*ORD *God walking in the garden in the cool of the day, and Adam and his wife hid themselves from the presence of the L*ORD *God among the trees of the garden. Then the L*ORD *God called to Adam and said to him, "Where are you?" So he said, "I heard Your voice in the garden, and I was afraid because I was naked; and I hid myself."* (verses 8–10)

Notice here that Adam's and Eve's full fellowship with God was now broken. They hid from God because they were naked. A separation began. No longer were they free and comfortable in their relationship with God. Also something else new developed. Adam's and Eve's guilt-conscious, disobedient hearts began to express themselves in the thing we call fear. It was their first emotional response after the Fall. From this experience, shame, guilt, inferiority, and insecurity became constant enemies of man.

> Disobedience brought separation.

When Adam and Eve sinned, the effects did not stop with them. Because Adam was the earthly father of the human race, every person after him was born into this fallen state of sin.

Therefore, just as through one man [Adam] sin entered the world, and death through sin, and thus death spread to all men, because all sinned. (Romans 5:12)

Adam's sin opened the door for us to know good and evil. From this, fear resulted. Now all mankind has experienced and will experience fear.

Let's see what happened next to Adam and Eve.

Then the LORD God said, "Behold, the man has become like one of Us, to know good and evil. And now, lest he put out his hand and take also of the tree of life, and eat, and live forever"; therefore the LORD God sent him out of the garden of Eden to till the ground from which he was taken. So He drove out the man; and He placed cherubim at the east of the garden of Eden, and a flaming sword which turned every way, to guard the way to the tree of life. (Genesis 3:22–24)

Remember that before the Fall, Adam and Eve knew no fear. They had open fellowship with God, their Father, and free access to the Tree of Life, or eternal life. However, after succumbing to Satan's temptation and accepting him as a new source of information, they became separated from God and trapped in bondage to the devil. He became their new father.[1]

> Adam and Eve first experienced fear after the Fall.

Remember, as we read earlier in Genesis, God had warned that eating from the Tree of Knowledge of Good and Evil would result in death. Before this, man would have lived forever, but with the Fall came the process of dying, eventual physical death, and eternal spiritual death. This is why God had to prevent Adam's and Eve's access to the Tree of Life. God did not want mankind to live forever in this fallen state.

In the Fall, Adam and Eve moved from relating to God as their spiritual Source of information to the devil. With this, man transferred his citizenship from the kingdom of Light to the kingdom of Darkness, and fear became one of the first by-products. (See Figure 1, p. 24.)

The Good News

That's the bad news. The Good News is that God loves man too much to leave him in this fallen, fearful state! Hallelujah!

For God so loved the world that He gave His only begotten Son, that whoever believes in Him should not perish but have everlasting life. (John 3:16)

---

1. See John 8 for a further explanation of unredeemed men and women having the devil as their father.

God sent Jesus to redeem us and give us once again free access to the Tree of Life, or eternal life. Jesus declared,

> *He who has an ear, let him hear what the Spirit says to the churches. To him who overcomes, I will give the right to eat from the tree of life, which is in the paradise of God.* (Revelation 2:7 NIV)

Jesus said that, if we overcome, we will have the right to eat from the Tree of Life. Who or what must we overcome, and how? God's Word tells us,

> *So the great dragon was cast out, that serpent of old, called the Devil and Satan, who deceives the whole world; he was cast to the earth, and his angels were cast out with him. Then I heard a loud voice saying in heaven, "Now salvation, and strength, and the kingdom of our God, and the power of His Christ have come, for the accuser of our brethren, who accused them before our God day and night, has been cast down. And they overcame him by the blood of the Lamb and by the word of their testimony, and they did not love their lives to the death."* (Revelation 12:9–11)

We overcome the devil by the blood of Jesus, which He shed on the cross for us, and by the testimony of our new life with Him.

Jesus also said, *"Blessed are those who wash their robes* [in the blood of Jesus], *that they may have the right to the tree of life and may go through the gates into the city* [eternal life in heaven]" (Revelation 22:14 NIV). Jesus restored us to a right relationship (righteousness) with God, so man may now fellowship with Him once again.

> *As one man's trespass* [one man's false step and falling away led] *to condemnation for all men, so one Man's act of righteousness* [leads] *to acquittal and right standing with God, and life for all men.* (Romans 5:18 AMP)

By accepting Jesus, we transfer our citizenship from the kingdom of Darkness back to the kingdom of Light. (See Figure 1, p. 24.) God, instead of the devil, becomes our new Source of knowledge, wisdom, and information. As Paul wrote:

> *For this reason also, since the day we heard of it, we have not ceased to pray for you and to ask that you may be filled with the knowledge of His will in*

all spiritual wisdom and understanding, so that you may walk in a manner worthy of the Lord, to please Him in all respects, bearing fruit in every good work and increasing in the knowledge of God; strengthened with all power, according to His glorious might, for the attaining of all steadfastness and patience; joyously giving thanks to the Father, who has qualified us to share in the inheritance of the saints in light. For He delivered us from the domain of darkness, and transferred us to the kingdom of His beloved Son, in whom we have redemption, the forgiveness of sins. (Colossians 1:9–14 NAS)

God becomes our Father as He adopts us back into His family.

Even so we, when we were children, were in bondage under the elements of the world. But when the fullness of the time had come, God sent forth His Son, born of a woman, born under the law, to redeem those who were under the law, that we might receive the adoption as sons. And because you are sons, God has sent forth the Spirit of His Son into your hearts, crying out, "Abba [Daddy], Father!" Therefore you are no longer a slave but a son, and if a son, then an heir of God through Christ. (Galatians 4:3–7)

> **We can live without fear.**

We can now walk in fellowship with God our Father through Jesus Christ, experiencing His liberty and no fear: *"Where the Spirit of the Lord is, there is liberty"* (2 Corinthians 3:17 KJV). Jesus said,

Do not seek what you should eat or what you should drink, nor have an anxious mind. For all these things the nations of the world seek after, and your Father knows that you need these things. But seek the kingdom of God, and all these things shall be added to you. Do not fear, little flock, for it is your Father's good pleasure to give you the kingdom. (Luke 12:29–32)

The Effects of the Fall and Redemption of Man

In Figure 1 on the following page, you can see that when Adam and Eve disobeyed God and sinned in the garden of Eden, their Fall plunged them and

The Effects of the Fall and Redemption of Man

Kingdom of Light

Kingdom of Darkness

The Fall →

Kingdom of Light	Kingdom of Darkness
God is loving, nurturing Father	Satan is warring, devouring father
Free access to Tree of Life	Prohibited access to Tree of Life
Eternal life	Eternal death
Fellowship with God	Separation from God
Prohibited access to Tree of Knowledge of Good and Evil	Free access to Tree of Knowledge of Good and Evil
God is Source of information	Satan is source of information
Liberty in God	Bondage to Satan
Naked and not ashamed	Shame and guilt, producing false cover-ups

No Fear ← **Jesus** **Fear**

Figure 1

all mankind from God's kingdom of Light into a new world. Adam's and Eve's first emotional response to their new life in the kingdom of Darkness was fear. However, through the finished, redemptive work of Jesus on the cross, man may return to the kingdom of Light. Now, through Jesus, we can become adopted sons and daughters of God. After accepting Jesus as our Savior, we are entitled to all God's blessings, including the right to live without fear.

Guard against Temptation

If you are a Christian, these are your new rights. However, you still live in this fallen world, where Satan rules as the *"god of this world"* and his children dwell: *"In whom the god of this world hath blinded the minds of them which believe not, lest the light of the glorious gospel of Christ, who is the image of God, should shine unto them"* (2 Corinthians 4:4 KJV).

> Never return to Satan's bondage once Christ has set you free.

The apostle Paul warned early Christians that Satan would try to draw them back into his kingdom. He wrote, *"But I am afraid that just as Eve was deceived by the serpent's cunning, your minds may somehow be led astray from your sincere and pure devotion to Christ"* (2 Corinthians 11:3 NIV). You must remember that Jesus already paid the price to free you from Satan's bondage, so do not go back. Focus on God, not the devil, and look to Him as your Source of information. *"Stand fast therefore in the liberty by which Christ has made us free, and do not be entangled again with a yoke of bondage"* (Galatians 5:1).

Be ever watchful not to release your God-given rights and blessings, which Jesus bought for you. *"Be sober, be vigilant; because your adversary the devil walks about like a roaring lion, seeking whom he may devour"* (1 Peter 5:8). You must not fear the devil, his information, or his cohorts. The Bible declares: *"You are of God, little children, and have overcome them, because He who is in you is greater than he who is in the world"* (1 John 4:4). You have no reason to fear. Jesus shed His blood and gave His life for your freedom and victory. It's time for you to reign as a king in life with no fear.

For if because of one man's trespass (lapse, offense) death reigned through that one, much more surely will those who receive [God's] overflowing grace (unmerited favor) and the free gift of righteousness [putting them into right standing with Himself] reign as kings in life through the one Man Jesus Christ (the Messiah, the Anointed One). (Romans 5:17 AMP)

You see, when you accept Jesus as your Savior, you don't simply receive a pass to escape hell and eternal death. Jesus gives you a new life on earth, one like Adam's and Eve's before the Fall. He brings you back into fellowship with God and opens the door to all His blessings. Reign in this life as a king. There is no need to fear.

What Is Fear?

It is clear now that God does not want us to fear evil. Although we might understand this truth, it is often difficult not to fall into fear. Why? To answer this, let's examine what fear actually is.

If you refer to a dictionary, you are likely to find a clinical explanation of fear, describing it as an emotional and physiological response of animals and human beings to dangerous stimuli or impetuses. In this regard, fear is a life-saving instinct.

But think back to our earlier discussion about the garden of Eden. Before the Fall, fear did not exist, nor did danger. Afterward, though, fear and danger became a common part of man's existence. Now, in this fallen world, fear is a benefit only when it produces a life-saving thought or extra strength to flee a dangerous situation or fight an aggressor. For example, if you are in the middle of a road and a huge tractor trailer is speeding toward you, you will likely experience fear. The physiological results of that fear will help you to spring to safety. Then, when the danger passes, the fear also should fade.

Fortunately, not many of us find ourselves in this type of dangerous situation very often. For the most part, our fears are unfounded. Generally, the probability that our worst fears

Fear did not exist before the fall of man.

will come true is very remote. However, even if our fears are likely to manifest, constant fear is a destructive force. It is not physically, mentally, or spiritually healthy for you if, in the normal course of life, your mind becomes inundated with a constant sense of uncertainty, dread, and worry. In 1 John 4:18, which we will look at further, the apostle John stated, *"Fear involves torment."* Your heavenly Father does not want you to be tormented! This type of fear steals the joy of the Lord from you and drains you of your ability to trust in God.

In *Make Fear Bow,* we are dealing with destructive fears. In future chapters, we will discuss how you must guard your life, identifying your motives and the impetuses to which you respond. Otherwise, if you do not understand what moves you, anything can grab hold of you. Being controlled by unknown forces is not God's plan for your life, because your enemy will take advantage of you to destroy your dreams and even your very life.

Our Real Enemy Authors Fear

A fearful mind-set comes from Satan, our enemy.

Who is our enemy? Many would describe an enemy as one who is poised to attack them, such as in a war. However, we must see that our enemy is not people, nations, races, religions, or cultures. Instead, our enemy is a mind-set, a constant pattern of thought that uses aggression and tyranny to suppress us into bondage. This mind-set unleashes great fear and suffering. Now, based upon our study of the events in the garden of Eden, we know the true enemy behind this mind-set is Satan. He uses his demonic spirits or fallen angels, about which we read earlier in Revelation 12:9, to deceive people and cause them to fall into fear. Let's examine this point further.

The apostle Paul declared, *"For God has not given us a spirit of fear, but of power and of love and of a sound mind"* (2 Timothy 1:7). Here we see that fear is a demonic spirit. Paul very clearly taught that God does not intend for His children to live with this spirit.

What Is a Spirit?

First, we must understand what a spirit is. As you read the Bible, you see phrases, such as *fallen angels, unclean spirits, evil spirits, familiar spirits, demons, devils, the spirit of fear,* and *the spirit of bondage.* The definitions of these are easy to understand, because they all come from the same source. An angel is simply a messenger[2], so a fallen angel is a messenger that communicates information from a source contrary to God's Word. That source is the devil! *Demon* is the Greek word *daimon* from the root *da,* which means "to know." Therefore, a demon is "a knowing one."[3] This type of being communicates knowledge from its source, the devil.

The book of Hosea states: *"My people are destroyed for lack of knowledge…. The people that doth not understand shall fall"* (Hosea 4:6, 14 KJV). Do not allow the ignorance of others to bring destruction to your doorstep. Jesus promised that *"you shall know the truth, and the truth shall make you free"* (John 8:32).

Spirit of Bondage versus the Spirit of Adoption

To the Romans, Paul explained, *"For you did not receive* [from God] *the spirit of bondage again to fear, but you received the Spirit of adoption by whom we cry out, 'Abba* [Daddy], *Father'"* (Romans 8:15). This verse takes us a little further. Not only is fear a demonic spirit, but we see more specifically it is also *"the spirit of bondage."* This means fear literally comes to bind and hold you in its limiting, controlling grip.

Remember, we studied earlier that in the kingdom of darkness, man is in bondage to Satan. Fear is the evidence or symptom of a cause, which is spiritual bondage. Bondage results in fear. In other words, *if you experience fear, it means you have bondage.* In that area of your life, you are operating in the kingdom of darkness!

> The devil enslaves, but Jesus liberates.

2. James Strong, *Strong's Hebrew and Greek Dictionaries* (Cedar Rapids: Parsons Technology, 1996), G32.
3. W. E. Vine, *Vine's Expository Dictionary of Old and New Testament Words* (Nashville: Thomas Nelson, 1997), p. 283.

Now, please do not misunderstand. You can be a Christian and still experience fear. If you are fearful in certain areas of your life, it simply means you have not experienced the freedom in those areas that Jesus bought for you. You are still in bondage to the devil in those parts of your life.

In the Greek, *bondage* means "slavery."[4] Think about it. Anything that causes fear has an element of bondage or slavery, which controls your life to some extent. When you are a victim of fear, you come under the control of an ungodly spirit that shackles and oppresses you. Thus, you become its slave.

These are not experiences from the kingdom of Light! Jesus has come to set you free. He said,

The Spirit of the Lord is upon Me, because He anointed Me to preach the gospel to the poor. He has sent Me to proclaim release to the captives, and recovery of sight to the blind, to set free those who are downtrodden, to proclaim the favorable year of the Lord. (Luke 4:18–19 NAS)

Abba Father Lovingly Adopted You

A vast gulf exists between the spirit of bondage, which results in our fear and paralysis, and the fellowship we have with God as His children. Let's examine this point closely, because it is one of the most profound keys to eliminating fear! At first, it may seem complicated, but it is very simple.

In 2 Timothy 1:7, God's Word contrasts *"a spirit of fear"* with *"power... love and...a sound mind."* In Romans 8:15, fear is set in opposition to our adoption by our heavenly Father. How are these elements related? What does fear have to do with love and adoption? Here is the answer: Fear is inversely related to our understanding of God's love and adoption. In other words, as one increases, the other decreases:

- The more we realize God loves us and has adopted us, the less fear we have.

- Alternatively, the more fear we experience, the less we truly understand and believe that an all-powerful, loving God has adopted and is caring for us.

---

4. *Strong's Hebrew and Greek Dictionaries*, G1397.

Grasping this revelation is the key to over-coming fear. Do you see that experiencing God's acceptance, care, and love causes you to lose every hook of fear in your life? Now, it should be clear that fear is not the major issue you must reckon with. Instead, you need to focus on knowing and believing in God's love for you. This is how you make fear bow. God's love is so powerful that it drives away all fear!

> The more we understand how much God loves us, the less we will fear.

The Bible clarifies this connection further when it says,

> *There is no fear in love; but perfect love casts out fear, because fear involves torment. But he who fears has not been made perfect in love. We love Him* [God] *because He first loved us.*　　　　　(1 John 4:18–19)

Notice that if we fear, we have *"not been made perfect in love."* Do you see how fear and love are inversely related? God's perfect love casts out all fear, which is an instrument of torment, because His love generates calm and certainty. Since your spirit is born of God's love, it is very secure because it thrives on that love. The key to being free of fear, then, is to rest in God's perfect love.

Consider a six-week-old baby, for example. How much fear does that child have? None. He has no reason to fear. The baby knows only the nurturing womb and then the loving care from his mother, father, or whoever is attending to his needs. That child has absolutely no ability to care for himself. He totally depends on his caregivers. This is why the baby has no fear.

You see, fear in our lives stems from thinking we must care for ourselves, while knowing we do not have the necessary power to provide everything we need. A tiny baby is powerless to care for himself, but he has no fear because he knows his caregivers will provide for all his needs. He has known nothing else.

Read Romans 8:15 again: *"For you did not receive* [from God] *the spirit of bondage again to fear, but you received the Spirit of adoption by whom we cry out, 'Abba* [Daddy], *Father.'"* When earthly parents want to adopt, they make a decision to do so. Likewise, your heavenly Father has chosen you to live at this point in history to be His child.

In love, God has chosen us, and He will care for us.

Just as an adopted child fearlessly accepts that Mom or Dad will care for him, we, as Christians, can fearlessly believe that our Daddy God is caring for us. We have not been thrown to the wolves to fend for ourselves. Our lives are not under our own direction. It is not up to us to make everything happen. No, we have a loving Daddy God, who has adopted us and cares for us. Because of this, we need not be afraid that our next steps will take us off course, causing us to crash in life.

Not long after babyhood, we move from trusting in and relying on the nurturing, loving care of our parents to believing that we have to depend upon ourselves to meet our needs. Somewhere between infancy and first grade, we transfer our dependence to ourselves; we lose some of that loving assurance with which we started life. For instance, I have prayed for children who were very nervous about beginning first grade. They were afraid because they were about to step from the ordinary into the unknown. You see, fear not only attacks us in precarious situations, but also in environments that are new to us.

In much the same way as little children become fearful, we often turn from trusting in our loving heavenly Father to thinking that we are totally responsible for our own well-being. We forget how much the Father loves us.

This revelation has transformed many lives. One woman, in particular, had a traumatic fear of crossing the Delaware Memorial Bridge, a twin-span bridge that connects New Jersey and Delaware. Her fear was so intense that every time she drove to the bridge, she had to park her car on the side of the road at the entrance. The police, who govern that bridge, had to drive her car across the bridge for her.

Now, why did this immense fear of bridges and heights grip this woman? Because she was relying on her own ability to keep herself safe while on that bridge. However, because she knew she was powerless to prevent any accidents, fear resulted.

Then one day while I was teaching on the love of God, this woman suddenly received the revelation that God's love casts out all fear. It changed her life! The next time she was ready to drive across that bridge, instead of succumbing to fear, this woman experienced the powerful presence of the Spirit of God. He showed His great passion and love for her.

The woman's response was this: "God would never let me be blown off the bridge because of how much He loves me." That was the last time she experienced any fear crossing that bridge. For many years now, this woman has been traveling back and forth practically every week—without even sweaty palms.

Resolve that, because of God's love, you will break your dependence on yourself so that you will no longer live under the grip of fear. Rest in the fact that God's love is far greater than the enemy's ability to induce fear in your life. As a Christian, you are part of the family of God. Stay near your heavenly Daddy. Jump into His lap every day! Then, from that powerful perspective, live and pray without fear.

You Have God's Authority

What gives you the ability to live without fear? The book of Ephesians declares that you are seated with Christ at the right hand of the Father:

> *And what is the exceeding greatness of His power toward us who believe, according to the working of His mighty power which He worked in Christ when He raised Him from the dead and seated Him at His right hand in the heavenly places, far above all principality and power and might and dominion, and every name that is named, not only in this age but also in that which is to come. And He put all things under His feet, and gave Him to be head over all things to the church, which is His body, the fullness of Him who fills all in all.…And raised us up together, and made us sit together in the heavenly places in Christ Jesus.* (Ephesians 1:19–23; 2:6)

Look at it this way. In the spirit realm, you are at the right hand of God, crying out, *"Abba, Father."* Legally entitled to everything in heaven, you have the absolute right to know God's will and purpose for your life without fear. You are a citizen of heaven with rights to heaven on earth. Freedom from fear is your right, because heaven has no room for fear. Jesus has conquered this foe.

When you stand on earth as God's ambassador, do not be afraid. You don't have to submit yourself to the devil's tactic of fear, and Jesus never uses

> ## In Jesus' name, command fear to go.

fear as a tool to force you to obey Him. Therefore, do not allow fear to paralyze you. Instead, make fear bow in Jesus' name!

You see, fear is bound to stay with you unless you make it go. Yes, you can actually make fear go! You can eliminate it, not by your own power, but because God provides you with the authority to do so in Jesus' name. In your human frailty, you do not have the power and authority to remove fear, but in Jesus' name you do! His name is above all names, including the name of fear. The Bible declares:

Therefore God also has highly exalted Him and given Him the name which is above every name, that at the name of Jesus every knee should bow, of those in heaven, and of those on earth, and of those under the earth, and that every tongue should confess that Jesus Christ is Lord, to the glory of God the Father. (Philippians 2:9–11)

Decide now which authority you will you walk in, man's or God's. To whose authority will you submit? I encourage you to look beyond man-made stipulations, walk in God's purposes, and make fear bow.[5] If you have fear, know it is not from God. He did not give a spirit to His children that limits, restricts, binds, and enslaves. No! Living in fear is not God's will for your life. He has designed you to be free. The spirit of fear should not cripple and torment you. If you are a Christian, you have a different Spirit, which is the Spirit *"of power and of love and of a sound mind"* (2 Timothy 1:7). That's the Spirit of God residing inside you! Instead of living in fearful torment, wouldn't you rather have a sound mind, knowing that a powerful God loves, cares for, and dwells in you? It's true. Now is the time to believe the Word of God and make fear bow!

That's easy to say, you might be thinking, *but hard to do. I want to believe this, but fear is still gripping me. How can I get free?*

It is not difficult to become free of fear. If you are a Christian, fear has no right to torment you. The only way fear can operate in your life is if you open

---

5. Read more in my book *Your Liberty in Christ* about the freedom Jesus bought for you. See my book *Conquering Your Unseen Enemies* regarding this principle of authority.

the door to it. You simply need to close the doors to the causes of fear. Then you can live in peace and fulfillment.

Recognize the Causes of Fear

I began to seek the Lord, asking Him, "What specifically causes people to fear? Why does fear exist in the lives of redeemed Christians?" To defeat this debilitating enemy, we must know what gives it the power to operate in our lives. Then we can know how to remove this hindrance. While I was in London, spending approximately one hundred hours in prayer, studying, and meditating on the Scriptures, God spoke to my spirit about the causes

God designed you to live in freedom.

of the destructive kind of fear. He revealed that fear is rooted in four major factors.

Cause #1: Trusting in the Flesh

As I studied and prayed about the topic of fear, the first cause I discovered is relying on what the Bible calls the *"arm of flesh"* (2 Chronicles 32:8). This is man looking at and trusting in his own limited ability to cope or deal with challenges. In other words, he trusts in what he can do to fix matters on his own. This response eventually creates fear.

Cause #2: Believing Information as It Naturally Appears

The second cause of fear is believing information as it naturally appears. This is accepting negative information from the natural environment. This may include reports such as an insufficient checkbook balance, a high credit card statement, or a doctor's prognosis about the sure progression of a fatal disease. Believing this type of information produces fear.

Cause #3: Sensory Reactions of Fear

The next cause of fear comes from the way a person's five senses react to natural information. We have seen many examples of sensory reactions inducing fear, such as *seeing* on the news the collapse of skyscrapers; *hearing* screaming people and sirens; *smelling* smoke; *tasting* something metallic in food; and *touching* an unusual lump under one's skin. These kinds of sensations naturally induce fear.

Cause #4: Entertaining Evil Imagery

The fourth cause of fear I learned is allowing an evil spirit to produce its imagery in the mind. These mental pictures that the enemy suggests may be either enticing or frightening. For example, they may include alluring sexual visions that, at first, appear to be harmless, but can lead to devastating consequences. Or they may be horrible scenarios that envision a loved one being killed in an accident, one's house or office building catching on fire, contracting cancer, being fired from a job, having a home or car repossessed, people speaking negatively behind one's back, and a myriad of other false impressions. Rehearsing either lustful or dreadful images results in fear.

Throughout the following chapters, we will discuss in detail these four causes, uncovering how these elements create fear, as well as how to overcome them. Understanding this will enable us to break free from fear's bondage so that we can live victoriously in God's promises!

Let's pray together:

Father, thank You for delivering me from the kingdom of Darkness into the kingdom of Light. Jesus, thank You for laying down Your life to give me free access to the Tree of Life, eternal life. You have restored my relationship with our heavenly Father. Jesus, help me to guard diligently this precious gift. You are greater in me than he who is in this world. I refuse to surrender any area of my life to our enemy, the devil. Help me to remain free.

Father, You have not given me the spirit of bondage to fear. Therefore, I bind the spirit of fear in Jesus' name. It must bow to the authority Jesus has given to me. I refuse to let fear and faith cohabit in my heart. Fear will not rule over my life, in Jesus' name.

I know and believe that You love me, Father, and that You have adopted me as Your child. Because You are providing for all my needs, I have no reason to fear.

God, You alone are my Source of information. I will not listen to any voice contrary to Yours. Thank You for the power and anointing of Your Word, which I expect to transform my life. Thank You that I can perceive the realm of Your Spirit and break the effects of fear from my life. In Jesus' name, Amen.

CHAPTER THREE

TRUSTING IN THE FLESH

Everyone faces limitations in life, such as in education, relationships, finances, abilities, communication, and perceptions. When you come to such an obstacle, at whose resources do you look to determine if you will overcome it? Does fear set in when you try to predict how you will fare? Why does this happen? The Bible has a very simple answer.

One of the major causes of fear is relying on what the Bible calls the arm of flesh. This is man focusing on and trusting in his own abilities to cope or deal with challenges. You can recognize if you are operating in this arena when you look to yourself or a natural plan, not God, to solve your problems or to deal with life's situations. Then, if and when things do not work out the way you desire, you feel frustrated and limited. This produces fear, and you do not move forward.

As we walk through this chapter, I believe you will break free of this unseen but familiar bondage or limitation that has caused you to fear!

Where Is Your Trust?

Earlier, I explained that I took about two thousand prayer requests to London with me. One was from a young man who was completing his master's degree. While attending school, he had worked in a fast-food restaurant the entire time. Now, he was ready to look for a job that would make use of his education. However, great fear set in. Because the man had never been employed in the field of his training, he believed he could not succeed in it.

Consequently, he requested prayer to overcome the fear of even applying for jobs in line with his education. After I prayed for him, he was able to send out many résumés. However, he soon accepted a job that was *not* in his field. To my knowledge, this man still has a job that is not in his field.

Do you see how powerfully destructive fear can be? What caused such a highly qualified individual to feel so inadequate that he jeopardized his entire future? The answer is in whom he trusted.

The prophet Jeremiah warned: "*Thus saith the* LORD; *Cursed be the man that trusteth in man, and maketh flesh his arm, and whose heart departeth from the* LORD" (Jeremiah 17:5 KJV), or as the *New International Version* of the Bible reads: "*This is what the* LORD *says: 'Cursed is the one who trusts in man, who depends on flesh for his strength and whose heart turns away from the* LORD.'"

When we trust in our natural capabilities and strengths to deliver us, we place our confidence in and give our allegiance to ourselves instead of God. In doing this, our hearts depart from Him.

Additionally, depending on the arm of flesh causes us eventually to come to the end of ourselves. At some point, everything we have and are will not be enough. Although this young man had earned a master's degree and was well prepared to take a job in his field, he was not able to turn his knowledge into a quality life. You see, we can utilize all our abilities, talents, mental prowess, knowledge, access to information, business acumen, communication skills, persuasive personalities, influence, authority, strength, positive attitudes, and finances. Yet we can still have no answers. Despite our own giftedness, we can find it impossible to bring our dreams to reality.

> **Have you come to the end of yourself?**

Sometimes we may even seek others who apparently have what we need to solve situations, but no man's arm of flesh is enough. After all our mental gymnastics and examination of everything, we will not be able to figure out what to do next. We will have mentally worked every angle, thought it all, tried it all, and done it all. Yet the wall of defeat will still loom ahead with no way through it. Confusion, frustration, exasperation, discouragement, and fear are the end results. Most of us live in this arena without realizing it.

Are you facing challenges today in which you have exhausted all your faculties and the natural avenues within your reach? Is there nothing more you can do? Do you have a spiritual work to accomplish but are coming up short in the natural realm? Maybe you desire to move forward in your vision, but you cannot see how.

What Can God Do?

When you come to the end of yourself, you might have a fleeting thought that maybe God can help. Then your mind rehashes all the mechanisms of how you have tried to make things work already. After all that, you ask, *What can God possibly do? I've tried everything.*

The answer to that question is *He is the answer!* God is everything you need. When you arrive at a dead-end, an apparently futile position, God is your ultimate solution. After failing to effect a change, you need to seek Him. Many people eventually recognize this truth and step over the threshold of fear into God's kingdom. Although this is wonderful, it would have been better if they had done it right away. Painful consequences exist for relying on the arm of flesh instead of on God.

You see, when people recognize their flesh is not powerful enough to solve their challenges, they often turn to futile activities. Some virtually destroy themselves through drug or alcohol abuse, sexual promiscuity, irresponsible financial behavior, a lawless lifestyle, bankruptcy, eating disorders, or other unhealthy, diabolic habits. When irreparable repercussions set in, many finally turn to God for help. The same God they abandoned becomes their only solution at this point of grief and regret.

I urge you not to reach that point of depletion before you seek God. If, instead, you place your confidence in a God whose competence knows no bounds, you can live in peace. Then, if a loved one receives a disappointing medical diagnosis or another negative challenge arises, you will not have to rely on your meager capabilities. Otherwise, if you do not trust God as your

Source, you will pay too great a price. You will encounter obstacles in the way of His blessings and plans for you, prolonging their fulfillment or even aborting them.

As we will read, when Moses and many of the Israelites trusted in themselves, they failed to enter the Promised Land. They aborted God's plan for them. It is time to benefit from others' experiences. You do not have to learn from your own failures! Turn to God now.

Do Not Curse Yourself

Remember, when you trust in the arm of flesh, the Bible says you are cursed. We read this earlier in Jeremiah 17:5. This is the result of bypassing God and relying on your own competence.

The next verse explains the effects of this curse: *"For he shall be like a shrub in the desert, and shall not see when good comes"* (verse 6).

Have you ever sensed that good things are happening all around you, but you are missing out? If so, this is an indication of self-trust! You see, when you rely on your own abilities and resources, the Bible says that you will not recognize good when it comes to you. Why? You are looking at what is *not* working in your life so much that you overlook the good that's there! You grope aimlessly in darkness and do not receive God's gifts, although they are fully accessible. You become oblivious to His blessings.

> Can you see the good in your life?

There is more bad news here. Let's continue this passage: *"For he shall be like a shrub in the desert, and shall not see when good comes, but shall inhabit the parched places in the wilderness, in a salt land which is not inhabited"* (verse 6).

When you align your confidence with the flesh, you step into the curse of the Word, resulting in barrenness and futility. All the while, you are blind to God's blessings that surround you. Consequently, you abandon your dreams and calling. Paying great attention to what is wrong in your situation, you don't see God, who stands ready, waiting to empower you to accomplish your purpose.

Can the Arm of Flesh Feed Thousands?

Let's consider the miracle of Jesus feeding the crowd of five thousand men, plus women and children.

And Jesus, when He came out, saw a great multitude and was moved with compassion for them, because they were like sheep not having a shepherd. So He began to teach them many things. (Mark 6:34)

After Jesus had been teaching a while, the disciples realized the people needed to eat. They asked Jesus to let the people go get food.

When the day was now far spent, His disciples came to Him and said, "This is a deserted place, and already the hour is late. Send them away, that they may go into the surrounding country and villages and buy themselves bread; for they have nothing to eat." (verses 35–36)

However, Jesus was not bound by the disciples' plan. Knowing they did not have enough to feed the crowd, nonetheless, He commanded His disciples:

"You give them something to eat." They [the disciples] said to him, "That would take eight months of a man's wages! Are we to go and spend that much on bread and give it to them to eat?" (verse 37 NIV)

Taking their eyes off Jesus and His power, the disciples looked to their own supplies and finances. Defeated by their limited resources, they could not conceive a plan to solve their current crisis. The arm of flesh was simply not enough, but Jesus had more than the arm of flesh!

But He [Jesus] said to them, "How many loaves do you have? Go and see." And when they found out they said, "Five, and two fish." Then He commanded them to make them all [the crowd] sit down in groups on the green grass. So they sat down in ranks, in hundreds and in fifties. And when He had taken the five loaves and the two fish, He looked up to heaven, blessed and broke the loaves, and gave them to His disciples to set before them; and the two fish He divided among them all. So they all ate and were filled. And they took up twelve baskets full of fragments and of the fish. Now those who had eaten the loaves were about five thousand men. (Mark 6:38–44)

When the disciples decided to focus and rely on their own capabilities, they quickly became exasperated in all their operations. They were incapable of understanding Jesus' plan to feed so many with what appeared to be an inadequate supply of food. They stifled their faith by trusting in themselves.

> Where's your focus— on what can go wrong or on God?

Like the disciples, we eventually give up in despair when our natural abilities and resources are unable to match the tasks facing us. We focus on every possible thing that can go wrong instead of God's promise and faithfulness to provide the way. Remember, the Bible celebrates God as a Provider. When you reach a hopeless dead-end, you can be sure that God is faithful to keep His promises to provide for you.

Is Your Life Like a Desert or an Oasis?

The reward of such trust in God is clear in the next verses of Jeremiah:

Blessed is the man who trusts in the LORD, and whose hope is the LORD. For he shall be like a tree planted by the waters, which spreads out its roots by the river, and will not fear when heat comes; but its leaf will be green, and will not be anxious in the year of drought, nor will cease from yielding fruit. (Jeremiah 17:7–8)

When you trust and hope in the Lord, although years of drought may dry up everything around you, those frustrations and limitations will not touch you. In fact, you will not even notice them. Instead, all you will see is abundance. You will continue to expand, increase, flourish, and develop fruit. I like the sounds of *that* kind of abundance! Don't you?

Contrast this image of blessing and fulfillment with the picture of those who trust in man, as we read earlier in the verses from Jeremiah. Remember, those who trust in themselves are cursed and live in a parched, desolate wilderness. They cannot see good even when it comes. Their lives are miserable.

Terrorism, rumors of wars, a poor economy, a plunging stock market, sickness, unemployment, and other traumas can surround you. However, if you are planted in the anointing of God, you will still know God's goodness. On the other hand, if you plant yourself in your natural strength, you will never see the goodness God has all around you, because the bad will seem to outweigh it. Now, think about that for a moment. Which kind of person are you?

Let me ask this another way. Does your life resemble an oasis or a desert? If it's a desert, you can change that! The choice is yours:

- Trust in God and flourish, or look to yourself and wither away in fear.
- Focus on God-sized prospects, or limit yourself to your natural expectations.
- Achieve big dreams with God, or sit on the sidelines of life with dashed hopes, longing for a taste of "the blessed life."

I encourage you to reject the arm of flesh and trust in the Lord! Then you can see His goodness and receive His direction for your life: *"Trust in the LORD with all your heart, and lean not on your own understanding; in all your ways acknowledge Him, and He shall direct your paths"* (Proverbs 3:5–6).

The Arm of My Flesh Could Not Buy the Building

I have had great opportunities to practice this principle in our ministry. For example, when we bought the first building for our ministry headquarters in New Castle, Delaware, it was a $4.5 million project. We had to raise a million dollars in cash as a down payment or else the bank would not loan us the remaining portion to buy it. This was an excellent price, and we needed the property. However, I had a tremendous amount of fear about needing a million dollars. It is a small amount to me now, after all God has produced to reach the world for Christ, but it was the first time I needed an amount this large for His vision.

The one million dollars was not simply something nice to have. No, we would lose the building if we did not get it. Pressure mounted as I tried to calculate where I could find that much money. The deadline grew closer and closer every day. It began to affect me negatively. During my early morning prayer, as I walked around the building and prayed, I had to rebuke fear continually!

> ## Fear multiplies when we trust solely in ourselves.

What was happening to me? Why was fear coming against me so strongly? Because I had opened the door to fear by trusting in my own strength, trying to figure where *I* could get a million dollars in cash. My brain was working overtime trying to solve this challenge, but I was coming up short of the goal. I had exhausted everything I could do and had come to the end of my natural ability. I did not know what else to do.

You see, we expend our energy, mentally trying to calculate the answer, instead of relying upon the Lord Himself, who is there the entire time to help. Have you ever experienced this kind of mental gymnastics when embarking on a vision from God? Have you reached the end of your ability? If you are human, then you have!

After exhausting all my revenue, resources, and ideas to raise the money, fear set in. It had a debilitating effect upon my life. I realized I was bound and found myself suffocating, paralyzed with no apparent way out. The more I pondered the evidence of my inability to raise the money, the greater my fear factor became and the more I began to question my ability to achieve God's dream. From this mind-set of snowballing fear, I prayed to God for help. However, it was as if my prayers were hitting a brass ceiling. It was like throwing a ball attached to a string—the ball kept returning to me. My prayers were ineffective. I was powerless to solve the challenge.

To gain victory, I had to put all this into the proper perspective. Finally, I realized that obtaining this building was not dependent upon me. It was dependent upon God to do what He had promised me. After all, it was *His* vision!

The Holy Spirit ministered to me through a Scripture verse that has changed my life. It has become one of my favorites. He said to me, *"Fear not, for I am with you; be not dismayed, for I am your God. I will strengthen you, Yes, I will help you, I will uphold you with My righteous right hand"* (Isaiah 41:10).

I love this Scripture. As I meditated on it and prayed this verse aloud, I broke through my bondage of fear. My faith soared. Suddenly I saw where God was—He was with me! I understood the answer to my fear: "God is with me!" It is not, "You can do it, Gary." The answer, I realized, to overcoming my fear was this: "Fear not, for God is with me. Don't be dismayed, for He is my God. He will strengthen me. Yes, He will help me. Yes, my God will hold me up with His righteous right hand!" After focusing my faith on God's Word, my confidence soared in Him and His Word—not in my ability to make things happen.

Then I started declaring, "God, a million dollars to You is nothing. After all, that's hardly interest on a day's income for You!" I broke free from the fear, and, within a day, I received an amazingly creative thought from God to raise the million dollars. Literally, He had me believe for people to create wealth, and they did! They miraculously created a million dollars and donated it to the ministry. Within ninety days, we had one million dollars in cash, settled the deal, and bought the property. Hallelujah!

The creative answer to this challenge was available to me the entire time. However, as we read earlier in Jeremiah, I could not see the good around me because I was trusting in myself. I was too focused on the bad situation, since my flesh was unable to meet the goal. Instead, I had to trust God, so I could break through my mind-set of fear and see the good He had already provided. Only then was I in a position to receive the wisdom about how a million dollars would flow into this ministry.

I had had good reasons why I could not raise this money to achieve God's dream. It seemed impossible because, in my flesh, I did not know His answer. You see, God does what we do not expect because if we had thought to do it, it would be our flesh working it. Instead, He receives the glory when He does what is impossible for us to do! This is how God operates.

That was our ministry's first building on eighteen acres. Since then, God has provided a total of nearly thirty acres with the other buildings we have purchased. After the first million dollars, the next million was easy to believe

> **When you move past fear, the devil can't stop you.**

God for. The second one was for the television studio to begin the School of Biblical Studies. I received only one offering in our church for it. Afterward, a group of people came forward with the rest of the million dollars to fund the entire project! When we built the television studio and began the Bible schools, we were able to pay cash for it all!

Why was there such a great contrast between these two instances of raising a million dollars? Because our enemy, the devil, knows that if we can break through our first barriers to cross the threshold of fear, he will be unable to stop us from the next ones. Once we see God move in our lives, it is much easier to believe He will do it again. After the first breakthrough, who can stop us the next time?

I encourage you to persist in pursuing your God-given dreams, but reject the thought that it is dependent entirely on you to achieve them. Realize that God has not called you to fear. Instead, He has called you to break free from every bondage! You can do it because your God is with you to help, strengthen, and uphold you! Hallelujah!

The Arm of Your Flesh Cannot Heal

Even in ministry, many people depend upon their own strength. In fact, this is one of the greatest obstacles people face in their personal ministries.

I often see this when I take people to minister on the mission field. Fear strikes their hearts as they encounter foreign environments with situations they have never faced before. For example, I once lined up about 150 people with leprosy and other serious diseases, and I instructed my mission team, "Now, go get them! Hallelujah! Pray for their healings in Jesus' name." The team had to believe God for creative miracles, such as ears to grow back, faces to be filled in, and eyeballs to form and pop into eye sockets!

Some people on our mission team complained, "You're expecting me to go and believe God for *that?*"

"Well, yes," I answered. "That's why we're here."

They had to break past their thresholds of fear, because if they focused on the milky gobs where people's eyes should have been, they would not even pray the prayer of faith. They would not begin to believe God for miracles. Instead, they would say, "I am going home. These people are in bad shape." As our mission team obeyed God and prayed for these desperate people, great miracles resulted.

> Breaking through the first barrier of fear makes each victory easier.

You see, fear is one of the first spirits that attacks when you launch out to do the exploits of God. However, if you can simply overcome it, God will move in glorious ways! This has happened to me. It has happened to God's people throughout time. It will happen for *you!*

God Goes with You to Your Promised Land

The book of Deuteronomy chronicles some of the experiences the Israelites encountered after they escaped the tyranny of their Egyptian captors. Under the leadership of Moses, they wandered in the wilderness for forty years after fleeing Egypt. Unsure of their future, the Israelites struggled to believe God's promise that He was bringing them into a great, flourishing land. For four decades, this people followed God's pillars of cloud by day and fire by night.

During the Israelites' long journey, a new generation was born in the wilderness. These younger ones had no direct knowledge of their parents' bondage in Egypt or of their very brief visitation of the glorious Promised Land. They had only their parents' testimony and God's promise of a future new home some day.

Continually, during their wearisome wanderings, the new generation heard their parents complain about the food God was providing. The older generation forgot the burden of bondage from which God had delivered them. Instead, they murmured,

> *Who will give us meat to eat? We remember the fish which we ate freely in Egypt, the cucumbers, the melons, the leeks, the onions, and the garlic; but*

now our whole being is dried up; there is nothing at all except this manna before our eyes! (Numbers 11:4–6)

Lacking gratitude for all God had done for them, they grumbled and failed to trust Him.

> Fear hinders God from working freely in our lives.

Constant fear of the unknown and their enemies repeatedly impeded God's eternal plan for the Israelites' lives. You see, we offend God and limit His ability when we express fear. Our fear implies that we serve a small god and that we question God's utmost supremacy. Psalm 78, for instance, recalls how the Israelites missed God's blessings because they continually mistrusted and disobeyed Him. The Word says, *"Yea, they turned back and tempted God, and limited the Holy One of Israel. They remembered not his hand, nor the day when he delivered them from the enemy"* (Psalm 78:41–42 KJV).

In fact, these fathers of Israel trusted in the arm of flesh so much that God finally vowed that their generation would not enter the land He had promised to them.[6] This is why they wandered for forty years in the desert. However, God agreed to allow *their children* to enter the Promised Land instead of these fearful parents. Likewise, since Moses had trusted in the arm of flesh in a particular instance, God forbade him entry into the Promised Land as well.[7]

Then, in Deuteronomy 31, the new generation of Israelites was about to enter the land God had promised to their fathers. According to the Word of the Lord, they had seen the death of their parents' generation. Their leader for forty years was still alive but about to die. At this point, Moses, now 120 years old, began preparing the new generation for his death and their subsequent entry into the long-awaited Promised Land.

God reaffirmed His commitment to serve as the shield for the children of Israel in the midst of dangerous enemies and futility. He also challenged their faith. Here, through Moses, God spoke to Joshua, whom He had chosen to replace the aging Israelite leader. He said to Joshua,

---

6. See Deuteronomy 1:19–36 and Psalm 95:10–11.
7. See Numbers 14:26–33; 20:2–13.

And the Lord *shall give them* [Israel's enemies] *up before your face, that ye may do unto them according unto all the commandments which I have commanded you. Be strong and of a good courage, fear not, nor be afraid of them: for the* Lord *thy God, he it is that doth go with thee; he will not fail thee, nor forsake thee.* (Deuteronomy 31:5–6 KJV)

Notice here that God admonished Joshua to *"fear not."* Why should Joshua *"be strong and of a good courage"?* As God later repeated, He promised to go *with* Joshua and not fail or forsake him. In fact, He would go *before* Joshua also: *"And the* Lord, *he it is that doth go before thee; he will be with thee, he will not fail thee, neither forsake thee: fear not, neither be dismayed"* (verse 8 KJV). God knew of the Israelites' (and all mankind's) tendency to lean on fleshly strength and ingenuity and fall into fear.

The younger Israelite generation desperately needed a "fear not" motivation, so they would not fall into this temptation as their fathers had. Moses encouraged them with their victorious past: *"And the* Lord *shall do unto them as he did to Sihon and to Og, kings of the Amorites, and unto the land of them, whom he destroyed"* (Deuteronomy 31:4 KJV). God not only promised them the land, but He also promised to be with the Israelites as they went to possess it.

Are Your History, Present, and Future Imposing Limits?

As we discussed earlier, this new generation of Israelites had no firsthand knowledge of their people's past blessings. Think about it. Their history was simply a story they had heard. Their future was another story, and they had nothing in the present to boast in. Their lives looked dry, barren, and devoid of a hopeful future. They had no physical evidence that God would keep His promise. Yet, despite their circumstances, He led them into their Promised Land.

Does *your* history seem like a dream and your future even more of a dream? Do you find yourself on the edge of a future you do not know if you can enter because nothing in your

> Does a past failure have you bound in chains of fear?

past or present indicates it is possible? Are you caught in this state of limbo with nothing to boast about in your present?

Maybe you have allowed past failures and hopelessness to enslave you. Perhaps you failed in a past business venture and now fear you will always fail at business. Maybe you failed your algebra test and fear you can never pass an algebra test again. If your first marriage was a disaster, you may fear you can never have a successful marriage.

Possibly the past failures and challenges of other people haunt you. Maybe your elder brother or sister was unsuccessful in law school, and you fear similar failure, although in your spirit you are convinced you should be a lawyer. Perhaps you watched in horror as the terrorists attacked the United States in 2001. Do you now feel vulnerable, recognizing that civil authorities who failed to detect and abort those events cannot prevent every possible attack in the future?

> **God will never fail you.**

No matter how your past, present, and future appear, God will go with you to bring you into your land of promise. He will not fail you. He is all you need! The Israelites' parents may have failed them occasionally, but God never did. Likewise, your earthly parents or other significant people in your life may have failed you, but your heavenly Father will not. Regardless of your circumstances, do not be discouraged. God will not abandon you despite the magnitude of your trials, distresses, or dilemmas. Nothing is too big for Him. However, for His purposes to manifest in your life, you must be fearless!

You Are Abraham's Seed

You might be thinking, *Yes, but that's the Old Testament. Those promises are not for me today.* That is not true. As Christians, we can claim the promises God made to the Israelites. Why? Because the Bible says we are Abraham's seed. *"And if you are Christ's, then you are Abraham's seed, and heirs according to the promise"* (Galatians 3:29).

You see, God made a covenant of blessing with Abraham, the father of the Israelites, and we have inherited this covenant. Here is what God said to Abraham:

I will make My covenant between Me and you, and will multiply you exceedingly....I will make you exceedingly fruitful; and I will make nations of you, and kings shall come from you. And I will establish My covenant between Me and you and your descendants [seed] after you in their generations, for an everlasting covenant, to be God to you and your descendants [seed] after you. Also I give to you and your descendants [seed] after you the land in which you are a stranger, all the land of Canaan [the Promised Land], as an everlasting possession; and I will be their God.

(Genesis 17:2, 6–8)

God has extended His covenant with Abraham to include us. In fact, as Christians, we have an even *better* covenant: "*But the ministry Jesus has received is as superior to theirs [the Israelites'] as the covenant of which he is mediator is superior to the old one, and it is founded on better promises*" (Hebrews 8:6 NIV).

You have the right to every promise in the Bible, including those in the Old Testament. Look for a promise in God's Word to help you face every challenge.

God Is All You Need

Do you need strength? No matter how seemingly impossible the challenge is, do not fear, for God's Word promises that He is the strength of your heart: "*My flesh and my heart fail; but God is the strength of my heart and my portion forever*" (Psalm 73:26). Joel 3:10 reiterates our ability to be strong: "*Beat your plowshares into swords and your pruning hooks into spears; let the weak say, 'I am strong.'*" You are strong in the Lord!

There is absolutely nothing to fear because God Almighty is *for* you. The Bible says if He is for you, who can possibly be against you? "*What then shall we say to these things? If God is for us, who can be against us?*" (Romans 8:31).

Are You Alone?

Among the prayer requests I took to London was one from a wife who had worked to put her husband through college as a full-time student. They had delayed having children so that he could finish his graduate degree. For two years, the wife feared that her husband, who now had an education and social grooming, would think he was free because of not having the tie of children. She asked for prayer because she was afraid that, in his place of success, he would leave her for someone else. This, in fact, did happen. The first wife had sacrificed her life for this man, yet when he achieved his success, he dumped her. She felt very alone and abandoned. The tragedy was that what she feared the most came upon her. *"For the thing I greatly feared has come upon me, And what I dreaded has happened to me"* (Job 3:25).

> **You are not alone.**

Do you feel you are facing life alone? Think about it. Do you seem isolated in the midst of conflicts? Maybe you sense an overwhelming loss or helplessness in your life. If so, you may have become frustrated, desperate, and maybe even suicidal, because you fear you have nowhere to turn. You may believe you have prayed every conceivable prayer and done everything possible. Yet nothing seems to solve the crisis. God has a better way.

Let's settle a few issues right now. What has God promised to you in the verses we have looked at so far? Do you remember?

+ He is going before you to lead you in the way you should go.

+ He is going with you to face your enemies.

+ He is your strength.

+ He is your help.

+ He will uphold you with His right hand of righteousness.

+ He will not fail you.

+ He will not forsake you.

+ He is for you. Who can stand against you and almighty God?

+ He will destroy your enemies.

+ He will bring you into your promised dream.

That's what God will do *with* and *for* you! It is not true that you are alone or that you have to depend upon yourself.

Now, what did God say your response should be? *Fear not* as you go in to possess His promises. The reason He has recorded all these verses in the Bible is so that His people will not be afraid. If you can understand in your spirit the power of these promises, you will break the great bondage that causes fear. It is one of the primary revelations you need to defeat the spirit of fear.

> **Making God's promises your own will defeat the spirit of fear.**

When you grasp the fact that God Himself is with you, you gain courage and strength to proceed. Why? God is all-powerful and will not lie. His Word says, *"God is not a man, that he should lie, nor a son of man, that he should change his mind. Does he speak and then not act? Does he promise and not fulfill?"* (Numbers 23:19 NIV). God will do what He has promised. Do you believe Him?

No matter what you face, including financial, physical, and emotional challenges, God is with and for you. If you are in the midst of a calamity or are about to do something God has told you to do, know that you are not by yourself. If God has spoken it, how on earth could anyone or anything annul it?

What If I Fail?

Maybe you are thinking, *That's a nice thought, but didn't God promise to bring the parents of the Israelites into the Promised Land and then change His mind when they sinned? What if He changes His mind about me when I fail Him? I'm not perfect.*

No, you do not have to be perfect. If you fall, then you must sincerely repent in order to keep in close relationship with Jesus Christ. God declares in His Word: *"If we confess our sins, he is faithful and just to forgive us our sins, and to cleanse us from all unrighteousness"* (1 John 1:9 KJV).

"To cleanse us from all unrighteousness" means to restore us to a right relationship with God as if our sin had never existed. When you sincerely repent, Jesus erases your sin with His blood. A repentant heart is the key to staying

God blesses those who obey Him.

in the blessings and promises of God. You see, God plans blessings for those who obey Him and curses for those who do not. However, the Bible explains that God will reverse these plans based upon repentant or unrepentant hearts:

If at any time I announce that a nation or kingdom is to be uprooted, torn down and destroyed, and if that nation I warned repents of its evil, then I will relent and not inflict on it the disaster I had planned. And if at another time I announce that a nation or kingdom is to be built up and planted, and if it does evil in my sight and does not obey me, then I will reconsider the good I had intended to do for it. (Jeremiah 18:7–10 NIV)

Remember, the Israelite parents were stubborn and would not repent. Therefore, they brought God's wrath upon themselves. He gave them ample opportunity to repent so that He could bless them, but they refused.

Now therefore say to the people of Judah and those living in Jerusalem, "This is what the LORD says: Look! I am preparing a disaster for you and devising a plan against you. So turn from your evil ways, each one of you, and reform your ways and your actions." But they will reply, "It's no use. We will continue with our own plans; each of us will follow the stubbornness of his evil heart." (verses 11–12 NIV)

Failing to repent is not worth it. This is the only way God will not go with you and be for you. Therefore, when you miss the mark by sinning, quickly run to God in repentance. Then get back on the path to the vision He has planned for your life, and He will be with you again. Actually, *you* will be with *Him* again, because He did not leave you; you left Him. Remember, God promised that He will never forsake you.

Do the Word You Know

Do you have a dream in your heart from the Spirit of the Lord? Do you know beyond a shadow of a doubt that God has spoken it to you? Maybe you have talked about it to others or maybe you haven't, but you believe that God put it there.

Now, are you experiencing setbacks in that area? Are you questioning whether you should go forward because of so many challenges? Are you experiencing fear about even trying anymore, because the last time it did not work? Has your dream become a progression of failures? Does it continually appear as though you can do nothing about it? Maybe people have even told you, "That's the way it is. You'll just have to live with it, because nothing is changing." That is not true! God is going with you to help you to accomplish your dream!

> God will enable you to fulfill the vision He has given to you.

Think about your dream. What is it? Right now as you think about fulfilling your vision, is fear, due to your natural limitations, trying to grip you? Are you asking, "How will I ever do that?"

We have read God's answer to this question: *"Fear not."* It is that simple. As you make fear bow and trust fully in God, you will seize your dreams for the future if you keep a repentant heart! This is how you enter your Promised Land, your promised dream from God.

You might say, "I know the Scriptures. I've memorized them, and I confess them, but it doesn't look like anything is changing."

Well, fine. Then live them out, and fear not.

"I can't figure out how it will work."

Trust in the Lord, and fear not.

"This isn't my area of gifting."

Fear not.

"I don't have the finances to do what I want to do."

Fear not.

"I've said and done everything I know how to do, and my family situation still hasn't changed."

Fear not.

"I've confessed the Word of God over my body, but I'm still sick. The doctor says there's no hope."

Fear not.

You see, when you trust God, it is very important not to look at your past or present circumstances. Look beyond them to focus on God and His Word. Even after you exhaust every pathway to achieving your goals, do not be afraid.

Step over the Threshold of Fear

President Franklin Delano Roosevelt said just after the United States entered the Great Depression, "The only thing we have to fear, is fear itself." Fear is all that restricts you. Instead of succumbing to fear, know that your Father is a miracle-working God who will always safeguard, defend, and provide for you. He is with you and will bring you into the glorious future He has planned for you!

God is almighty and will operate and rescue you in ways that are beyond your thinking and comprehension. His Word tells us that He *"is able to do exceedingly abundantly above all that we ask or think, according to the power that works in us"* (Ephesians 3:20).

Live God's Best

Today, would you take new action if you knew for sure that God would be with and for you in it? Yes? Then why don't you take that action? Remember that the reason you can walk without fear is not because you can handle any challenges on your own. It is because He is with and for you. His Word promises it. That means it's true! Therefore, you can confidently take new action to live God's best.

God is with you and for you.

Personally, I trust that God is with me and for me in every situation. For example, if I had to handle this ministry by the arm of my flesh, I would not sleep well at night. If by myself I had to manage the hundreds of Bible Schools we have, run our church, handle all the mission programs, create books, and do everything else God has called us to do, it would be too much. Thank God that it's not me doing all this, but it is the Lord in me. *"I can do all things through Christ who strengthens me"* (Philippians 4:13). Hallelujah! Anchor your trust in Him. He will help you to accomplish His visions in your heart and life.

Make Every Fear Bow

It is time for you to make fear bow, so you can experience God's promises in every area of your life. Let's start with finances. Have you exhausted all your ability to figure out where to get money? Do you have objectives that you cannot imagine how to reach financially? This is when fear sets in.

Second, do you have family challenges? Have you prayed everything you should pray, believed everything you should believe, said everything you should say, and thought everything you should think? Yet do you still face the same challenges within your family? That's when bondage and fear come.

Do you have a decision about your future that you cannot see how to make? Do you have dreams and visions that you cannot figure out how on earth you will ever accomplish? Does it appear to be a futile attempt in stupidity even to attempt them? If so, you are at the threshold of fear.

I encourage you to do something now. Stand up and, with your finger, draw a line in front of your feet. On the other side of the line, I want you to look at what has been holding you back. Look at it. Maybe it is the fear of not having enough money, education, favor with people, physical or mental ability, or something else that has tried to limit you. Maybe it is the fear of loneliness, rejection, man's opinion, death, flying, speaking in public, or another fear. Whatever your hindrances are, look at them all. They have probably multiplied over the years.

> Identify your fears.

Now, let me ask you a question: Do you want to stay there—behind the line, stopped by your fears? Seriously, do you want to stay in bondage to those fears and limitations? If not, then you must do something. Act as if God is who He said He is. Trust that He will not fail or forsake you.

The Holy Spirit of God is stirring inside my spirit now. I know that He wants to work in every area of your life. Let me ask you another question. The Bible says God did not spare His own Son but sacrificed Him for your redemption. Why would He give you less now? Why would He desert you now?

> *What then shall we say to these things? If God is for us, who can be against us? He who did not spare His own Son, but delivered Him up for us all, how shall He not with Him also freely give us all things?*
> (Romans 8:31–32)

God loves you and promises to give you freely *all* things. That's everything—**all** things. Glory! This can be as small as saving two hours of time, or as big as children returning from the snare of the devil. It can be a small blessing of receiving a few extra dollars in your pocket to a big blessing of funding every dream and vision God has spoken to you. This promise includes *all* the things you are believing God for in your life!

Right now, I encourage you to open your heart to heaven. Take a moment with God to settle this issue of fear once and for all. Unburden yourself. Admit that you have drained your personal resources and that all your efforts have held you down in fear. It's time to break this power of fear in every area of your life. Let's make fear bow in Jesus' name!

Pray this now:

Father, I have exhausted my ability. I have become exasperated in my own attempts to meet my challenges. Oh, God, forgive me for relying on the arm of flesh, for depending on myself, and for measuring my limited resources against the circumstances I face.

Today, I have come to a threshold, and I see what is limiting me: this power of fear. Lord, You have given me the ability to go over this threshold, to make a lie out of that which stands to limit me. By the power of the blood of Jesus, I put under my feet the spirits that have been assigned to withstand me. I thank You, my God, for the anointing that is here to lift burdens, break yokes, and release me from the restraint that fear has had on my life.

Father, as Your child, I will no longer submit myself to this bondage of fear. Help me not to rely on the rhetoric of uncertainty in my mind. I dismiss the thoughts of discouragement and impossibilities that pressure me over and over again. From now on, I look only to You, God—the one, true, unwavering Source of comfort and strength.

Father, thank You for Your promises. I know You are with and for me wherever I go. You will not fail or forsake me through the tribulations, trials, traumas, and distresses of life. You are upholding me now with the right hand of Your righteousness. You do not want me to be discouraged or give up. You are the strength of my life. I place my trust in You this day. I will not fear anything that comes against me. God, thank You for rescuing me from all my enemies, including fear. In Jesus' name, Amen.

Now, speak to the enemies who are limiting you. Declare this in Jesus' name:

I command fear to bow in the name of Jesus, because God is with me and for me. I will not be dismayed. Fear must release its hold on my life and bow in Jesus' name right now.

I command discouragement, doubt, cynicism, and pessimism to loose my life, for God is with me and for me. He is my joy and faith.

I say to weakness that I am strong, for God strengthens me.

I say to every attack on my life, the Lord is my protection. He is for me. You cannot stand against Him and me. I say to helplessness and hopelessness, the Lord is my help and hope. The Lord, who is with me and for me, helps me and gives hope to me.

Therefore, because of God, I am fearless and full of faith, hope, and joy. I am strong because He helps me. In Him, I am well able to break the power of this resistance. I will go on to receive and accomplish all that God has for me. In Jesus' name.

Now, I encourage you to think about what God wants to do with your life. What has He been speaking to your spirit lately? Right now, start praying for that vision to become clear to you. Don't worry about the details of how you will accomplish it. Don't succumb to fear. Simply pray the very things you perceive the Spirit of God is saying to you. Let them erupt from your heart. Pray that dream. Pray that vision. Pray that directive. Then close your prayer with these words:

Father, I commit my way into Your hands. I decide not to look at my own strength and ability to carry out this dream, vision, or directive from You. I look only to You, the Author and Finisher of my faith. You, Father, are the One who put it into my heart to do this thing. You will be the One to accomplish it in my life.

In Jesus' name, I will not bow to pain, difficulty, distress, discouragement, worry, or fear that might try to attack this dream. God, I fix my eyes on You as I make fear bow. I step over this threshold of fear, trusting that You, Father, will fulfill every promise You have given to me. I thank You that I can see my dream coming to pass because You are with me! In Jesus' name, Amen.

CHAPTER FOUR

BELIEVING INFORMATION AS IT NATURALLY APPEARS

What is your usual response when you receive negative information? For example, if a weather reporter announced that a hurricane or tornado was heading toward your town, what would you do? How would you respond if a doctor's report showed that you had an incurable disease? What if you received a letter saying you weren't hired for a job you confidently interviewed for? If you walked into a courtroom, would you be intimidated by the size of the room or the stern look on the judge's face?

Destructive fears are produced not only by trusting in the arm of flesh but also by believing information that comes from a natural source rather than from God. I call this natural information. Many people, including entire congregations, have allowed themselves to become weighed down by fear because they focused totally on how circumstances looked. This type of fear has significantly increased as people have glued themselves to their television sets, watching bombings, terrorist activities, shootings, rapes, robberies, and more, but it does not have to be. Seeing shouldn't necessarily be believing.

Natural Information Comes from Another Source

The media, doctors, accountants, attorneys, bankers, employers, and many others often are the bearers of bad news. When we become fearful after learning negative information, it means we are not relying on God. Instead, we are allowing ourselves to feed from a different source.

Earlier in our discussion of the Fall of man, we learned that when Adam and Eve ingested the fruit of the Tree of Knowledge of Good and Evil, they switched their source of information from God to the devil. Fear resulted as they fell into bondage to Satan. This bondage often comes from ingesting information from a natural source instead of God.

The Faith Walk

Have circumstances caused you to fear? Then, when you read the Bible, did you see your situation in a different light? For example, have you looked at your bank balance when it did not contain enough to meet your needs? If so, did fear try to overtake you? Then did you read in the Bible verses like these? *"And my God shall supply all your need according to His riches in glory by Christ Jesus"* (Philippians 4:19). *"But seek first the kingdom of God and His righteousness, and all these things shall be added to you"* (Matthew 6:33).

In circumstances that appear to be negative, you have the choice of accepting natural information from your environment or allowing supernatural faith to arise as you believe your heavenly Father's promises.

God is calling us not to act based on appearances alone. This principle applies in our workplaces, homes, doctors' offices, or wherever we go in every arena of life. The apostle Paul reminded the church that we are not to look at natural information:

> *While we do not look at the things which are seen, but at the things which are not seen. For the things which are seen are temporary, but the things which are not seen are eternal.*　　　　　　(2 Corinthians 4:18)

In other words, the natural realm, which we see every day, is temporary. It will not last forever. It will change. However, the spiritual realm of God's truth, which we cannot see with our natural eyes, is eternal and permanent. The truth of the spiritual realm has the power to change the short-term natural realm. As Paul said, *"For we walk by faith, not by sight"* (2 Corinthians 5:7).

As Christians, we are to measure appearances according to God's truth. If what we see with our natural eyes does not align with God's Word, then we are to walk by faith, believing God's Word will change our natural circumstances. This is the "faith walk" God calls His children to live. Fear results when we do not walk by faith and instead trust the information that the natural arena communicates. We listen and agree without consulting God's Word.

You may have heard the acrostic F.E.A.R.:

False

Evidence

Appearing

Real

This tool helps us to remember that false natural information often is portrayed as real. In other words, fear results from the manifestation of physical evidence that is false in relationship to God's promises. The devil uses natural information to tempt us to walk by sight (to believe in appearances) instead of walking by faith (believing in God's unseen promises). We can defeat F.E.A.R. by walking in faith, believing God's power will change our environments!

We Need a Healthy Realism

It is clear that God wants us to face every obstacle in our lives with faith. This does not mean, however, that we are to ignore bad circumstances and hope they go away. It does not mean that if the doctor diagnoses a disease, we simply throw away his prescription or refuse a plan of treatment, declaring, "No, I don't think I am sick." It does not mean that if our bank balances are negative, we continue writing checks, hoping money will flow into our accounts somehow. It does not mean that we say, "I'm not going to change my life at all just because some threat of danger exists somewhere. I don't think anyone is aiming at me. I'll be okay." This is not walking by faith. It is foolish living, like an ostrich with its head stuck in the sand.

> Living by faith involves being wise— not foolish.

You see, God expects us to live in what I call a healthy realism. We need to understand that we live in a natural world with real threats and dangers. However, we also know we have the Scriptures, which absolutely give us the right to move with authority by faith to change our environments. In other words, we must squarely recognize what we are facing in our lives, our country, and the world. Instead of denying that problems exist, we need to pray, speak the Word of God over these areas to bring them into alignment with His Word, and then do what God shows us to do about them.

For example, we acknowledge that we are sick, our checking accounts are overdrawn, or danger can strike us at any moment. We realize our circumstances are real. Yet we also know that God is able and desires to heal us, give us inspired ideas to raise money, and protect us from our enemies. We are not to ignore the facts, but speak His Word over them and move in His authority by faith.

You might be thinking, *Well, I don't want to think about negative things like this.*

I believe you need to. However, you should consider them from the context of God's sound perspective instead of from one induced by fear and uncertainty. You must know what the Word of God says about your environment and how to operate in it according to His will. For example, on the evening of Tuesday, September 11, 2001, after the terrorists attacked the United States, President George W. Bush pleaded in his remarks to the nation:

> Tonight, I ask for your prayers for all those who grieve, for the children whose worlds have been shattered, for all whose sense of safety and security has been threatened. And I pray they will be comforted by a power greater than any of us, spoken through the ages in Psalm 23: *"Even though I walk through the valley of the shadow of death, I fear no evil, for You are with me."* [8]

---

8. "'A Great People' Fights 'Despicable Acts of Terror'" NewsMax.com.
<http://www.newsmax.com/archives/articles/2001/9/11/210908.shtml> (25 May 2002).

The President recognized the extremely difficult situation we faced. However, he encouraged us with the Word of God, admonishing us not to walk in fear because God is with us. In the midst of our challenges, we are to focus on the Greater One who is with us.

The Challenge of the Information Era

As Christians, we must not fix our eyes on our apparent environment. However, for approximately the past forty years, this has become an increasing challenge in the United States and most of the free world. The reason is that we have been baptized into an era of information and are inundated by communications through radio, television, newspapers, the Internet, and more. Now we can sit in our living rooms, dens, or nearly anywhere and instantly access a tremendous amount of information. From ten thousand miles away, we can even watch events unfold in real time before our eyes.

Some of us glue ourselves to cable news channels or up-to-the-second news on the Internet. Tragically, these broadcasts have become the gospel of America. The problem is that they have little good news and repeat the same old bad news continually until more bad news unfolds. The media floods us with fear-inducing natural information. For example, how many times did you see the same picture from September 11, 2001, of the hijacked airplanes flying into the World Trade Center? Soon, you could think of nothing else. Your family and friends were talking about it, and everywhere you went, you heard conversations about that event.

Where do you get your news?

Constant feeding on this type of information without God's Good News can have a devastating impact on our spiritual, physical, and mental lives. The danger is that the images the media presents can seem far more truthful than many of the other sources of information we normally consider truthful—including the Bible! To resolve this conflict, sometimes we need to turn off the television, saying, "I've seen that picture enough. If anything else happens, I'm sure someone will notify me." In the days immediately following the terrorist attacks on September 11, 2001, even the media interviews with mental health professionals revealed that, to stay healthy, people need a break from the constant barrage of horrible images. Whether they knew it or not, these experts were prescribing a biblical principle!

> *Do not be anxious about anything, but in everything, by prayer and petition, with thanksgiving, present your requests to God. And the peace of God, which transcends all understanding, will guard your hearts and your minds in Christ Jesus. Finally, brothers, whatever is true, whatever is noble, whatever is right, whatever is pure, whatever is lovely, whatever is admirable—if anything is excellent or praiseworthy—think about such things. Whatever you have learned or received or heard from me, or seen in me—put it into practice. And the God of peace will be with you.*
> (Philippians 4:6–9 NIV)

Remember that we need to keep God as our Source of information and not rely on the devil's constant display of natural information. Then our heavenly Father's peace will guard our hearts and minds.

Calculated Pessimism Induces Fear

> A pessimist sees what is instead of what can be.

The danger of constantly feeding our minds with natural information is that we can begin to believe it is truer than God's Word. We can jump to the conclusion that nothing can change what we perceive to be true. Therefore, we give up and become victims.

When you accept this mind-set, you not only doubt what God says and His ability, but you also put your confidence in facts, figures, and calculations that try to prove He cannot perform His promises. This is what I call calculated pessimism. After evaluating your circumstances, your mind accepts the limitations of the apparent circumstances instead of relying on the limitless power of God. You spend your life explaining why things will not work. As a result, you cannot accomplish your God-given dreams. This is a dangerous pattern because it invites fear and insults God.

This fear factor emerges, for example, when you obsess about a doctor's negative diagnosis of an incurable disease or one with severe complications. Such natural appearances arouse hopelessness and result in fear. However, the truth in God's Word declares: *"By whose stripes you were healed"* (1 Peter 2:24), and, *"He sent His word and healed them, and delivered them from their destructions"* (Psalm 107:20).

Do not look at the natural information and fall into fear. God's Word declares that your apparent circumstances are only temporary. His promise of healing is included in the more than seven thousand promises He has given to us in His Word. When we face challenges, we must trust God by finding and standing on His promises. Believe in the power of His Word to change your circumstances!

Wait on the Lord

My family and I have witnessed God's healing power in our lives many times. One year I dislocated my left shoulder while skiing; afterward, it continued to fall out of joint from time to time. Whenever my arm went out of its socket, I could almost scratch my knee without bending over! Sometimes this happened while I was preaching. Each time, I had to pick up my arm, put it back in the socket, and go on preaching. When I picked up my briefcase with that arm, my briefcase stayed on the ground, and my arm lifted out of the socket. From all appearances of the situation, it was a mess.

One time when I flew back from Africa, I could not get my arm to go back into place. To fix it, I wedged my arm between two seats and asked a man to jump on me to push it in. He screamed when he did it. I felt bad for him, but at least my arm went back into the socket. Hallelujah!

He said to me, "Gary, I don't think you should be taking these trips with your arm like this, because it stays out of joint for hours."

"Yes, I know," I said, realizing that when this happened, my shoulder became so swollen it was as if I were wearing a shoulder pad. Yet I knew God wanted me to minister, so what else could I do?

Finally, after many months of pain, I had an operation on my left arm and shoulder. However, after the doctor secured my shoulder with wire and screws, I was shocked to discover I had only a 30 percent range of motion! Now, I could hardly move my arm. Appearances were going from bad to worse.

God is not limited by circumstances.

I could have settled for that, but, praise God, His power changes our circumstances! One night we had All Night Prayer at our church. Suddenly, while I was worshiping God in the service, His power came through my shoulder and entirely recreated it, including my muscles! Now, I have 100 percent perfect mobility with no limitations, and I have never had a problem with it since! Not only that, God removed all the metal parts that the doctor had inserted. They are all gone, and we have the X-rays to prove it!

Wow! When God shows up, He does it right. In this case, however, He seemed to take a long time to do it. I had plenty of opportunity to fall into fear because of the appearance of my circumstances. Have you ever thought God was taking a long time to help you? I encourage you. Do not give up! God will do what He promised! Keep waiting on and trusting in Him.

If you trust in the natural facts instead, you bypass the living God. When you overlook God, you are inclined to adopt an attitude of calculated pessimism, because you begin to believe and accept things as they naturally appear. Then you settle for far less than God's intended best. However, when you place your trust in Him, you engage God's promises for your life. You rise above the narrow stipulations of information as they appear naturally and allow Him to rescue you. Remember, despite the circumstances, God is there to help you.

This is what Dr. Billy Graham meant when he spoke at the National Day of Prayer and Remembrance on September 14, 2001, after the terrorist attacks on the United States earlier that week. Dr. Graham said,

We've always needed God from the very beginning of this nation, but today we need Him especially….The Bible's words are our hope: "*God is our refuge and strength, an ever present help in trouble. Therefore we will not fear, though the earth give way and the mountains fall into the heart of the sea*" (Psalm 46:1–2)….My prayer today is that we will feel the loving arms of God wrapped around us, and will know in our hearts that He will never forsake us as we trust in Him.[9]

I have discovered that all mankind, including Christians, face calculated pessimism. Even Jesus' disciples, who physically walked with Him and saw His miracles firsthand, experienced this challenge. As long as we live in these earthly bodies, we will battle calculated pessimism. However, the more we trust God, the easier this fight becomes to win.

Jesus' Disciples Struggled with Calculated Pessimism

In the previous chapter, we studied the miracle of Jesus feeding five thousand men, plus women and children. There we saw how the disciples looked to the arm of flesh. In this chapter, we will examine how they also believed information as it naturally appeared. As a result, they walked in fear instead of faith. Calculated pessimism controlled their thinking.

Recall that Jesus was preaching to an immense crowd when His disciples expressed these concerns: It was late in the day, they were in a remote location, and the people needed food. Very aware of their environment, His disciples had evaluated the situation. They were unable to find a solution except to stop Jesus' ministry and send the people away to get food. Instead, Jesus told them to feed the five thousand men, plus women and children. Their reaction to this unusual instruction was laced with human skepticism.

Now, let's see how Jesus exposed what His disciples really believed:

Then Jesus lifted up His eyes, and seeing a great multitude coming toward Him, He said to Philip, "Where shall we buy bread, that these may eat?" But this He said to test him, for He Himself knew what He would do.
(John 6:5–6)

Here we see that Jesus was not concerned about how the hungry crowd would eat because He did not believe the natural information as it appeared.

9. Billy Graham's complete message can be accessed at
<http://www.billygraham.org/newsevents/ndprbgmessage.asp> (25 May 2002).

Instead, Jesus knew that in His Father's kingdom, there is no lack of resources. However, He wanted to test Philip to see if he would believe the natural information or look to Him for a solution.

When Jesus asked him where they would buy food, Philip responded: *"Eight months' wages would not buy enough bread for each one to have a bite!"* (John 6:7 NIV). Philip failed the test. His response revealed that he was believing only the natural information. He and the other disciples had checked their tangible resources and agreed, basically saying pessimistically, "We have calculated everything, and we are positive it's impossible to do what You ask, Jesus. There's no way!"

Is your vision God-sized?

The disciples did not understand what Jesus was doing. Fear gripped them. Although they were at the threshold of a miracle, they could not step over because they relied upon the apparent natural information. The F.E.A.R. factor emerged—**F**alse **E**vidence **A**ppearing **R**eal. When the disciples stared at the hungry crowd of five thousand men, plus women and children, they saw no possible way to feed them all.

+ It appeared that no one had enough food.
+ It appeared that it would be too expensive to go buy food for everyone.
+ It appeared that they could not get to the surrounding villages and back in time.
+ It appeared that the people would go hungry.

The evidence existed, but it was false, not by natural standards but by God-sized standards. The disciples did not consider the divine provision that comes by faith. Even these men who had walked with Jesus for several years believed natural appearances.

Remember how the miracle occurred here. Jesus told His disciples to check how many loaves of bread they had. Notice that He did not ask, "Do you have enough to feed the people?" He simply wanted to know if the disciples would hear Him instead of relying on the natural information. John's account reports:

One of His disciples, Andrew, Simon Peter's brother, said to Him, "There is a lad here who has five barley loaves and two small fish, but what are they among so many?" (John 6:8–9)

Do you see that Andrew passed the test? While he may not have understood how Jesus would do it, he did bring the meager food to His Lord. Andrew, in effect, said, "Jesus, we have evaluated the natural information, and we don't have enough to do what You ask. What we do have is this lunch of five loaves and two fish. I know it looks like a few crumbs compared to this crowd, but can You do anything with what we have?"

Yes, He could! That was enough!

I can picture Jesus responding, "Now, we can do something! You broke through the threshold of fear, and you are acting on what I spoke."

Jesus then took the five loaves and two fish and multiplied them:

He looked up to heaven, blessed and broke the loaves, and gave them to His disciples to set before them; and the two fish He divided among them all. So they all ate and were filled. And they took up twelve baskets full of fragments and of the fish. (Mark 6:41–43)

Everyone had enough to eat, and twelve baskets of food were left over. Their leftovers were more than they had started with!

You see, all Jesus needed from the disciples was a little faith, obedience, and a few crumbs of food. These were the seeds for a great miracle. That's all Jesus needs from us, too—a little faith, obedience, and not enough of what we need! Faith, the size of a tiny mustard seed; obedience; and the seeds of your need will produce your miracle. Think about that!

Jesus declared: *"If you have faith as a mustard seed, you will say to this mountain, 'Move from here to there,' and it will move; and nothing will be impossible for you"* (Matthew 17:20). Jesus also said, *"If you can believe, all things are possible to him who believes"* (Mark 9:23).

> Give Jesus your faith, obedience, and the seeds of your need, and watch what He will do!

Reject calculated pessimism today and trust in God. Obey Him despite what you see. This is how to have victory over the natural appearance of information. Remember, God is not subject to the limitations of the natural realm. Trust that if you need a miracle or if God plants a dream in your heart, He will provide the way to accomplish it!

Are you feeling like the disciples felt when Jesus commanded them to do something, but the natural information declared that they could not do it? Are you looking at a situation, an assignment, or a dream from God in your own life, and is your natural environment speaking negatively to you? The more it talks, are you becoming convinced that you cannot do what God has said? Is there no natural way to meet that need? Has the volume of negative reasoning increased, telling you it will not work, it's useless, it's hopeless, and it's not even worth trying? From the natural realm, does it appear that you absolutely cannot obey God?

If so, the Lord is testing you, as He did Philip. Do you realize He already knows what He will do in your life and how He will do it, but He wants to see how you will respond? God has miracles planned for you, but you must trust and obey Him despite the apparent circumstances! Will you pass His test? Will you believe the natural information, which has the power to induce fear? Will you allow a pessimistic attitude to set in? If so, it can cause you to lose your commitment to follow God and miss your miracle. However, you do not have to settle for this result. There is an answer for you, but you must not believe the natural information.

Old Testament Leaders Faced Calculated Pessimism

The Old Testament is filled with examples of God's leaders overcoming calculated pessimism as Andrew did when he participated in the miracle of feeding the five thousand. Let's consider several examples. In these stories we will see that when God operates, He usually does not work as we would expect.

Moses Used His Rod

Moses faced a crisis of belief when God charged him with the responsibility of leading the enslaved Israelites out of Egypt. At first, he hesitated when

God called him to this historic assignment. You may remember that earlier in Moses' life, he had failed when he relied on the arm of flesh to help his people. As a result, he killed an Egyptian, who was beating one of the Israelite slaves. Moses then hid the Egyptian's body. Let's read what happened afterward:

> *The next day he* [Moses] *went out and saw two Hebrews fighting. He asked the one in the wrong, "Why are you hitting your fellow Hebrew?" The man said, "Who made you ruler and judge over us? Are you thinking of killing me as you killed the Egyptian?" Then Moses was afraid and thought, "What I did must have become known." When Pharaoh heard of this, he tried to kill Moses, but Moses fled from Pharaoh and went to live in Midian.* (Exodus 2:13–15 NIV)

The first time Moses had tried to help the Israelites, they did not recognize God's call on his life. Of course, at that time, he was operating in the flesh and not in obedience to God. Nonetheless, Moses continued to remember the Israelites' negative attitude about him, and he feared his calling. He also fled in fear for his life.

Nearly forty years later, the Pharaoh who had sought to kill Moses died.[10] The Bible says that after hearing the Israelites' cries for deliverance from slavery, God instructed Moses to go back to Egypt to deliver them.

Moses calculated God's request and basically answered, "Lord, if I go back to free the Israelites, they will not believe me. I've done this before, and it didn't work." But God promised Moses, *"I will certainly be with you"* (Exodus 3:12). He wasn't sending Moses off alone to complete the assignment.

Still skeptical of the Israelites' response, Moses asked God who he should say had sent him. God told Moses,

> *"I AM WHO I AM." And He said, "Thus you shall say to the children of Israel, 'I AM has sent me to you.'" Moreover God said to Moses, "Thus you shall say to the children of Israel: 'The LORD God of your fathers, the God of Abraham, the God of Isaac, and the God of Jacob, has sent me to you. This is My name forever, and this is My memorial to all generations.'"* (Exodus 3:14–15)

---

10. See Exodus 2:23 AMP.

However, Moses held onto his calculated pessimism. He continued to insist that the Israelites would not believe him, so God gave a miraculous sign to Moses:

> *The* LORD *said to him, "What is that in your hand?" He [Moses] said, "A rod." And He said, "Cast it on the ground." So he cast it on the ground, and it became a serpent; and Moses fled from it. Then the* LORD *said to Moses, "Reach out your hand and take it by the tail" (and he reached out his hand and caught it, and it became a rod in his hand).*   (Exodus 4:2–4)

With this sign, God reminded Moses that while the task appeared practically impossible, it was divinely possible because God had ordained it.

To accomplish His vision, God asked Moses essentially the same question Jesus later asked of His disciples: "What is in your hand?" With that one question, Jesus tested their faith and obedience. What little they had was not enough for them to perform His assignment, but He wanted to know if they would hold on to it or surrender it to Him. Today, God asks the same of us.

Moses overcame his calculated pessimism, passed God's test, and went on to lead the Israelites from Egypt. With his rod, he parted the Red Sea, and all the Israelites escaped an otherwise sure defeat. By the power of God, Moses overcame the natural appearances surrounding him and, with no weapons, miraculously defeated Pharaoh and the Egyptian army. Moses used a rod in his hand, not his skill or military might, and God delivered a nation. With God, that's all Moses needed.[11]

David Used His Slingshot

David demonstrated a similar faith when he encountered Goliath. As you may recall, the Israelites and their enemies the Philistines gathered for battle. The giant Goliath came out from the Philistines to defy the ranks of Israel. He taunted them for forty days, demanding they produce a man to fight him. The Bible says,

> *When Saul [king of Israel] and all Israel heard these words of the Philistine, they were dismayed and greatly afraid....And all the men of*

---

11. To read more about Moses and his response to God in leading the Israelites out of Egypt, see Exodus 2–14.

Israel, when they saw the man, fled from him and were dreadfully afraid.
(1 Samuel 17:11, 24)

The appearance of natural information was terrifying. The king and all the Israelites calculated their circumstances and agreed they could not win.

However, David, still an adolescent who tended his father's sheep, sensed God's call for him to fight the giant warrior! He recalled God's miraculous hand upon him when a lion and a bear had come against his father's flock:

Moreover David said, "The Lord, who delivered me from the paw of the lion and from the paw of the bear, He will deliver me from the hand of this Philistine." And Saul said to David, "Go, and the Lord be with you!"
(1 Samuel 17:37)

Armed with a slingshot and five smooth stones, David marched off to fight the mighty giant. When Goliath saw David, he mocked the lad. The slingshot and stones David wielded appeared to be paltry weapons compared to the Philistine's size, strength, and weaponry. The natural information screamed that this boy did not stand a chance against the giant.

However, David replied to Goliath's cursing, saying,

"You come to me with a sword, with a spear, and with a javelin. But I come to you in the name of the Lord of hosts, the God of the armies of Israel, whom you have defied. This day the Lord will deliver you into my hand, and I will strike you and take your head from you. And this day I will give the carcasses of the camp of the Philistines to the birds of the air and the wild beasts of the earth, that all the earth may know that there is a God in Israel. Then all this assembly shall know that the Lord does not save with sword and spear; for the battle is the Lord's, and He will give you into our hands."
(verses 45–47)

Now that's faith! David went on to slay the giant. His faith and subsequent victory over Goliath defied natural expectations because all David had in his hand was a slingshot and five stones. Yet, with God that was more than enough to win the battle, which eventually led to David being proclaimed as the king!

The Word of God is true. This promise is for you, too!

"No weapon formed against you shall prosper, and every tongue which rises against you in judgment You shall condemn. This is the heritage of the servants of the LORD, and their righteousness is from Me," says the LORD.   (Isaiah 54:17)

Others in the Bible Used What They Had

The Bible abounds with accounts of faith-filled people overcoming natural information with supernatural inspiration from God—using what they had in their hands.

> With God, you always have enough to meet any challenge.

In Judges 15, for example, we read that Samson used what he had in his hand to kill one thousand Philistines. At the time, ropes bound him. Yet, as the Spirit of the Lord came upon him, the restraints fell off! Samson then picked up what was within his reach, the jawbone of a donkey, and killed one thousand of his enemies with it! You can overcome natural appearances.

Consider this example from 1 Kings 17. As the prophet Elijah came into the town of Zarephath during a drought, he saw a widow and asked her for a drink of water and a piece of bread. The woman explained that she was preparing to use the tiny bit of flour and oil she had left to cook one last meal before she and her son would starve to death. From the natural information, the widow's plight appeared hopeless, and so did the prophet's. You see, God had instructed Elijah that this widow would feed him. However, from all natural appearances, she did not have enough food for two people for more than a day! Yet the prophet had a supernatural message from God for her:

And Elijah said to her, "Do not fear; go and do as you have said, but make me a small cake from it first, and bring it to me; and afterward make some for yourself and your son. For thus says the LORD God of Israel: 'The bin of flour shall not be used up, nor shall the jar of oil run dry, until the day the LORD sends rain on the earth.'"   (1 Kings 17:13–14)

Well, that was good news, but the widow had to trust God and give His servant a meal from the last food she had on hand. Before feeding her son, she was to feed the prophet of God. This was a critical test of her faith.

What happened?

So she went away and did according to the word of Elijah; and she and he and her household ate for many days. The bin of flour was not used up, nor did the jar of oil run dry, according to the word of the LORD *which He spoke by Elijah.* (verses 15–16)

The widow's and the prophet's miracles came when they believed and obeyed the Word of the Lord. They used what they had in their hands despite natural appearances.

As another example, the Bible gives an account in 2 Kings 6 of some men who were building dwellings. As they were cutting down trees for the homes, the head of a borrowed ax accidentally flew off the handle and landed in a nearby body of water. The man who had borrowed the ax cried out to the prophet Elisha for help. The prophet asked where it had fallen. When shown where, Elisha cut off a stick and threw it in at that place. Immediately the iron ax head floated, and the man retrieved it!

The prophet Elisha used what was within his reach, a stick, to create the miracle his friend needed. It does not matter what we have in our hands. It matters only that we use it for God, obey Him, and believe!

Nothing in the natural arena appeared to work for any of these people of faith. However, God's Spirit had spoken supernatural information to their hearts, so they used what was in their hands. Although their weapons and tools were very weak, and the widow's food was a very small amount, in God all of it was sufficient to accomplish everything He wanted to do! God's supernatural power overcame all negative natural information.

> God turns weakness into strength; poverty into wealth; failure into success.

To achieve your God-given dream, you do not have to be a mighty warrior, successful business leader, wealthy retiree, or brilliant scholar. No, God uses weak, beggarly, and apparently unsuccessful people, whom no one else recognizes. He takes tools and things that everyone else discards and turns them into the very instruments of deliverance for His people. Always remember, you do not need the natural appearance of your circumstances in perfect order for your miracle. Simply believe the supernatural Word of God, obey Him, and use whatever He has put into your hand when He instructs you!

We Face Calculated Pessimism Today

Because of my passion to help developing nations, I served as a director in a humanitarian aid organization that feeds and services the underprivileged. Several years ago, the directors purchased and dedicated a cargo ship on behalf of the ministry. The ship, about the length of a football field, cost $16 million. Natural information initially discouraged us from purchasing it because we did not have the money. Many were doubtful that we could acquire the ship, but we did. When we dedicated it to the Lord, I looked at the ship and thought, *Hallelujah! Dear God, this is what faith produces in only a few months!*

Shortly afterward, we needed to buy a $12,000 forklift to move the grain and feed within the belly of the ship. The immediate reaction of some people was to calculate how much money we had and to conclude that we did not have enough to buy the forklift.

When one man asked, "Do you think we can pay for it?" the atmosphere was very negative.

Many people expressed their doubts, "No, we just bought the ship for $16 million. We can't come up with any more money." Their calculated pessimism was showing.

My response was the opposite. I thought, *My God, how calculated can we get? Lord, You just provided $16 million. What's a mere $12,000 compared to that? Surely You can give us the money for a forklift to go with the ship You provided!* I believed He would do it, and He did provide the funds for the forklift.

Appearances Try to Keep
You from Your Miracle

Let me ask you an important question: Have you calculated your natural resources and found that you do not have enough to obey God? You must realize that your natural resources are not designed for this because God is your Provider. His provisions will never fail. On the other hand, your enemy, Satan, tries to use your natural environment to lead you to abort your God-given dreams. He speaks to you through those circumstances. If you listen to Satan's voice in the natural information, you will fall into fear, doubt God's plan and provision, and lose your miracle.

You see, when the voice of the natural realm speaks to us, it can drown out God's supernatural voice. When our calculating human minds accept this information as it naturally appears, we allow its claims to bind us. This generates fear and prevents us from seeing past the natural limitations. Instead of listening to God's voice, our dependence on our limited resources stifles us. However, when we listen to His supernatural voice, we can look beyond the constraints of natural information.

Fear Blinds You from Seeing Your Miracle

Fear will tell you that you have already calculated and evaluated the situation, and you cannot win. Believing natural information will cause pessimism to run your life. Then you will not move forward over the threshold of fear's bondage toward your miracle. Fear can cause you to agree with other negative-thinking people who say, "We've counted all the money, we've gauged the distance, and it will not work." Have you had conversations of calculated pessimism like this in which people agree with you that your dream will not work?

You must realize that fear will prevent you from exploring your God-empowered potential, which is the ability to attain what appears naturally inconceivable. You see, fear will blind you from recognizing the seeds of your miracle. It will blind you from finding your loaves and fish and your miracle rod. Fear will prevent you from using a slingshot and stone to kill your Goliath or keep you from picking up a donkey's jawbone to slay your enemies. Fear will abort your miraculous provision of food and supplies. It will preempt you from finding your lost ax head. It will stop your ship from coming in, and then you won't even need a forklift!

If you live in fear, the pessimistic natural voice will tell you that you cannot succeed. It will keep you from looking for God's provisions. You will never know the visitation of God because you will continue to question what a boy's meager lunch could do for a crowd of thousands. You will be stuck wondering what a mere rod, slingshot and stones, or donkey's jawbone can do for you in the face of mighty weaponry. You will continue to presume that you will starve to death and never regain your losses. You will not be able to see how the little money you have can be enough to create the vision God has placed in your heart. Fear causes you to stop dead in your tracks and overlook the answer God has provided. In fact, you will not even look for it because you think, *Nothing can work.*

> Are you bowed in fear or making fear bow?

Are you allowing natural information to dominate your mind? Is it binding you to an environment and preventing you from moving on in life? Maybe you are afraid to seek help in an abusive marriage. Perhaps you are afraid to make a commitment because of the pain of divorce you have personally endured or have seen other couples go through. Maybe you have vowed never to fly again because you lost a loved one in a plane crash. Maybe you are afraid of driving on the highway because you once witnessed an accident or came close to being in one yourself. Are you bowed down in fear, not even looking for answers because of the natural environment? If so, it can shut down your life. Fear can debilitate you and create subsequent obstacles that can stop you from pursuing God's will for your life. You need to change your thinking to agree with God's plan for you.

Is God Calling You to Move out of Your Comfort Zone?

One of my staff came to me a few years ago, saying he had been in prayer for me. The Lord had told him I needed to buy the safest car possible. Now, my nature is to negotiate and spend the least amount possible. The type of car being suggested was very expensive! However, I recognized this was God's will for me. Despite the natural information, which told me not to spend that amount of money, I ordered a car from Florida and was not even able to test-drive it first, which was very unusual for me.

Before my new car had been driven one hundred miles, a person driving seventy miles per hour rammed her car into mine, completely crushing the passenger's side of my vehicle. It took forty-five minutes for the rescue workers to extricate me from the car!

If I had not overcome my mind-set of spending the lowest amount possible on cars and test-driving them, and if I had been in a more cheaply made car, I would not be alive today to write this book or share this story with you. Purchasing that more expensive car was way beyond my comfort zone, but I obeyed God's will for my life. By the way, that car was totally wrecked, and now I have another one like it. Hallelujah!

> **Is fear holding you back?**

Sometimes you need to step out from your comfort zone and normal mind-set in order to hear from God. What do you need to rethink? Every Monday, do you dread going to work because you hate your job? Have you counted the money, looked down the road, and thought you were too far along to change? Do you think you can do nothing about it? Who said you cannot quit? Who said you cannot apply for a job you enjoy? Who said you are bound there for the rest of your life?

One man had worked for many years in a company as a bookkeeper and office manager, but he was unhappy at his job. He dreamed of a better one, so he decided to attend night school to earn a degree in accounting at a nearby university. It took him thirteen years of steadily taking night courses until he graduated and earned his degree. In fact, he and his son graduated from the university at about the same time.

Afterward, the man's family thought he would change jobs to get a better one in his field. However, he was so afraid to leave his current job that he stayed in the same position at the same company. When he died many years later, he was still working in that same job, despite all those years of college to earn his degree.

If you do not like your job, why not quit? If you do not like the city where you reside, why not move? In situations like these, fear can cause you to stay in bondage. You remain confined to an environment or condition, afraid to trust God and move on.

You might be thinking, *Well, I can't quit my job. They are paying me.*

Many people are employed in the world. Why do you want to waste your time doing something you don't enjoy?

I'm afraid to leave it. I have security here.

Why? That job did not come from man. It came from God. The money they pay you comes from Him. If God is leading you to leave, He has another job lined up for you.

You might be worrying, *What if it takes time and I'm without a paycheck for a few months? I'd lose my house, car, and no telling what else.*

What did Jesus say? *"Man shall not live by bread alone, but by every word of God"* (Luke 4:4). If Jesus were walking on the earth today, He would say, "You shall not live from paycheck to paycheck, but by every Word of God." If a few months of interruption will make you lose everything, you probably do not own it anyway. You need to work toward getting yourself out of that debt. Speak God's Word into your finances and job. Allow Him to move in your life, so you can have a job you enjoy.

Maybe you have calculated the length of the journey to your dream and are saying, *My God, it's too far to go. I will starve to death before I get there. I will die in the wilderness along the way.* Wait. Listen for the voice of Jesus asking, "How many loaves do you have?" When you hear His quiet voice, it wakes up your spirit, so you can break through that barrier of fear. Bring what little you have to Jesus, and let Him move. Put your faith in Him, and you will see beyond natural appearances. Trust that God will perform His Word.

Gnosticism versus the True Gospel

God alone is more than anything you will ever need in the natural realm. He is whatever you need Him to be. He alone is more than sufficient. In Him, everything is possible.

Unfortunately, most Christians do not really believe this about God. Whether they recognize it or not, many believe a Gnostic gospel. This teaches that Christ plus something else equals fulfillment of the dream. They believe that happiness comes only with Christ plus some other support mechanism. The only way some Christians believe they can truly serve God is by combining their faith in Him with certain expecta-

> You do not need God plus something else.

tions. For example, they want Christ but also long for more money to make them happy. Maybe it is Christ plus marriage that will fulfill them, Christ plus a car and a house, Christ plus a vacation, or Christ plus knowledge.

Those who think this way set themselves up for a dangerous fall. When natural appearances indicate that the materials they believe they need, such as the finances to fund a vision, are not available, they fall into fear. They conclude that fulfilling their dreams is hopeless because they do not have the extra part they believe they need.

Gnosticism stems from the lie that God's Word needs something added to it to make it work. No, His Word alone is more than enough! This philosophy essentially defines God as inadequate. We do not need Christ plus anything. We need Christ alone. In Him dwells the fullness of the Godhead. The Bible declares about Jesus: *"For in Him dwells all the fullness of the Godhead bodily; and you are complete in Him, who is the head of all principality and power"* (Colossians 2:9–10). In Him, there is no lack. In Christ, we find all we need. His Word tell us,

> *As His divine power has given to us all things that pertain to life and godliness, through the knowledge of Him who called us by glory and virtue, by which have been given to us exceedingly great and precious promises, that through these you may be partakers of the divine nature.* (2 Peter 1:3–4)

All we need is in Him, but most of us have adopted the lie that we need something else in addition to God.

All we really need is Jesus Christ to touch the area of our insufficiency. He will produce whatever we need to carry out His vision. It is not necessary to have everything in place before we come to Him.

When it was time to buy that building for our ministry, I did not have enough money, but I had God. I did not need Christ plus a million dollars to buy it. The directors of the humanitarian aid organization did not have enough money to buy their ship and forklift, but God multiplied it. They did not need God plus millions to do it. The prophet Elisha had only a little stick with which to retrieve an iron ax head from the water, but he had God. He did not need God plus scuba divers to recover the lost ax head.

In the natural realm, the disciples, the widow at Zarephath, and the prophet did not need the Lord plus enough food. Andrew and the disciples had only five loaves and two fish in the midst of five thousand hungry men, plus women and children, but they had Jesus. During a drought, the widow of Zarephath had only a handful of meal and a little oil to feed the prophet Elijah, her son, and herself for many days, but she had God.

Moses, David, and Samson did not need God plus mighty weapons to defeat their enemies. Moses had only a rod in his hand as the Egyptian army pinned him and the Israelites against the Red Sea, but he had God. David had only his slingshot and five smooth stones as he confronted the mighty warrior giant, but he had the living God. Samson had only the jawbone of a donkey to kill one thousand Philistines, but he had God.

These men and women of faith took what they had in their hands, which was not enough, and believed God would use it to perform miracles as they obeyed Him. They attained what was naturally impossible. Therefore, we must not allow our natural circumstances to produce fear. As Jesus said to His disciples, "*With men this is impossible, but with God all things are possible*" (Matthew 19:26).

What Is in Your Hand?

What do you have in your hand to accomplish your dream? Don't see it as insufficient. See it as seed for your miracle. You already have everything you need to fulfill all God has said to you. That's Jesus! Put what you have into His hands and fear not! Then watch Him turn your lack into abundance. Watch Him turn your weakness into strength. Watch Him turn your natural circumstances into a supernatural miracle! Fear must bow its knee to Him, for He alone is more than enough. I Am is with you!

God has never gone back on even one of the promises He made to us. As a shepherd leads his flock to food and water, our loving Shepherd will supply all our needs. Hear His voice from heaven and step over the threshold of fear. You can hear His voice, if you listen. Jesus, the faithful Shepherd, said,

> *My sheep hear My voice, and I know them, and they follow Me. And I give them eternal life, and they shall never perish; neither shall anyone snatch them out of My hand. My Father, who has given them to Me, is greater than all; and no one is able to snatch them out of My Father's hand. I and My Father are one.* (John 10:27–30)

Trials or Temptations?

Maybe you have calculated your situation. You have added up the money, looked at the journey, and evaluated all the options. In all sincerity, everything in the natural realm indicates that your dream will not work. This is not a comfortable place to be. However, God sometimes takes you to those places. Why? He wants to see what's in you. At times, He tests your faith. This is different from the devil luring you off through temptation. The trials of your faith are precious to God. They establish how much you trust and love Him. His Word says,

> *In this you greatly rejoice, even though now for a little while, if necessary, you have been distressed by various trials, that the proof of your faith, being more precious than gold which is perishable, even though tested by fire, may be found to result in praise and glory and honor at the revelation of Jesus Christ.* (1 Peter 1:6–7 NAS)

> *Consider it pure joy, my brothers, whenever you face trials of many kinds, because you know that the testing of your faith develops perseverance. Perseverance must finish its work so that you may be mature and complete, not lacking anything.* (James 1:2–4 NIV)

Unfortunately, many of us fail here. We lose in the midst of our trials because we revert to fear and become paralyzed instead of going forward with our dreams.

> Count the cost, then move ahead with God's plan.

We should be saying, "Okay, I have counted the money. I have calculated the cost, and I don't have enough to make it. Now, let's go!"

Wait a minute, you say. *Didn't Jesus say to count the cost first?*

Yes, but let's look at that passage. He did not say, "Count the cost and quit." That's right. He meant that we should count the cost, and then do it. He said,

> *If anyone comes to Me and does not hate [in comparison with his love for Jesus] his father and mother, wife and children, brothers and sisters, yes, and his own life also, he cannot be My disciple. And whoever does not bear his cross and come after Me cannot be My disciple. For which of you, intending to build a tower, does not sit down first and count the cost, whether he has enough to finish it; lest, after he has laid the foundation, and is not able to finish, all who see it begin to mock him, saying, "This man began to build and was not able to finish."...So likewise, whoever of you does not forsake all that he has cannot be My disciple.* (Luke 14:26–30, 33)

Jesus instructed us here to count the cost of being His disciples, and then do it. He wants us as His disciples.

Jesus did not say, "Count the money, and if you have enough, do it." He wants us to do it, but we need to know what we must expend to achieve the goal. We need to be sure we can believe God for enough to build the whole building. It is important that we recognize the cost of faith before we begin the project. For example, when I bought the building for our ministry, I realized that we could not move into this complex with a $5,000 offering. No, I had to believe God for a million dollars. I had to be willing to expend my faith to believe Him for the full amount.

What Is God Speaking to You?

God places dreams and visions in His children's lives, but the devil uses the natural realm to deter us. Marital dysfunction, physical limitations, financial setbacks, and other areas of conflict and challenge develop, yet the Lord never neglects to fulfill one of His promises to us. We simply need to hear His gentle voice asking us, "What do you have in your hand?" We need to find the little boy with his lunch. Find the widow woman with a cruse of oil and a handful of meal. Find the rod, slingshot and stones, or the donkey's jawbone. Find the stick. You must find the inspired idea God has for you to create that vision He gave to you. Do not be afraid to look again at what you have. Find what God has been speaking to you about, and use it for His glory.

Get Rid of Nagging Conflict

Do you have a nagging conflict in your life like my dislocated arm? Are you afraid this challenge will hold you back from God's plans for you? Do not shy away from your conflicts. God uses them for His glory and to strengthen you. When He calls you, run into the battle with confidence. You see, every conflict you face strengthens you for the next battle. That's what happened to David. He first fought and killed a lion and a bear with his hands. The God who empowered him to do that could easily grant victory against the giant Goliath.

I believe He will do the same for you! Then your previous victory in conflict will become a stepping-stone to your next success. I have seen this happen countless times in my life. As I have mentioned, I have been in many environments that induce fear—including the physical realm, finances, my family, the social arena, the economy, and world travels. It never fails that the God who is with me is greater than any fear that comes against me. He gives the victory to me time and time again.

> Each triumph becomes a stepping-stone to the next victory.

That is the God who is with you today! Now, let's pray to break you free from the conflicts in your life. God wants to set you free. Declare these words aloud:

Greater is He that is in me than this fear. In Jesus' name, I serve notice to every stronghold that has bound me. I am not self-reliant.

My confidence is in Christ. I loose myself from the hold of fear in Jesus' name. Fear, you must bow your knee, for the I Am is with me.

I take authority over the fears, limiting factors, appearance of circumstances, bills, and pressures of life. In Jesus' name, you have no power, for God is with me. I break the besetting sin of discouragement and declare you must release your hold. You have no power over me in Jesus' name. I will not fear or be discouraged, for I Am is my God. Hallelujah!

Right now I receive strength in my spirit from my God. I receive health in my body. I receive the mind of Christ. My God upholds me in the palm of His hand, and no man can snatch me out.

Focus on the Lord

Oh, look to the Lord. Right now, where you are sitting, focus on Him for a moment. Recognize that He is the restoration of everything you have lost. He is the God who delivered you. He holds you in the right hand of His righteousness and cradles you in the palm of His hand. He will let no one take you from Him.

He is the God who bought you with His Son's blood, saying, in essence, "Since I sacrificed My own Son, will I not freely give everything to you?" Not only will He give everything, but *He is everything you need.* He is to you whatever you need Him to be. In fact, He is **all** you need! Hallelujah!

Receive His anointed power in your life now and pray His Word:

I will not listen to any voice contrary to the voice of the Good Shepherd. Jesus, You are the Good Shepherd. You go before the sheep. You lead me out. You make my paths straight. You level the mountains in my way. You lift up the valleys ahead of me.

God, in Your Word You said that I "shall go out with joy, and be led forth with peace." I trust You, and I stand on Your promises. You said You will restore my soul and lead me in the paths in which I should go. Your Word is a "lamp unto my feet, and a light unto my path" to guide me. You said, "I am the LORD your God, who teaches you to profit, who leads you by the way you should go." Thank You for showing me the way to go and for teaching me to profit.

You have "blessed us with all spiritual blessings in heavenly places in Christ." You promised whatever I put my hands to will prosper. God, You said I am like a tree planted by the rivers of water. When the heat and drought come, I shall not wither but will continually bear fruit in my season. You said whatever I do shall prosper. I trust Your Word.

Father, You declared no weapon formed against me will prosper, and every tongue that rises against me in judgment will be condemned. You said the weapons of my warfare are not physical, but, God, Your divine power is with me. You are with me! Thank You for being my defense. I hear Your voice from heaven and step over the threshold of fear because You are with me! You are with me! You are with me!

You said to Moses, "I AM WHO I AM," and You are that to me today. My God, You are Everything. You are the Husband to the husband-less. You are the Father to the fatherless. You are the Family to those with no family. You are the Comforter to the bereaved. You are the Strength to the weak. You are the Present Help to those in trouble. You are the Hope to the hopeless. You are married to the backslider.

You are my Deliverer. You are my Peace. You are my Safety. You are my Joy. You are my Life. You are Everything to me. You are Moses' Rod, David's Stone, Samson's Strength, and Elisha's Stick. You are Food for the disciples' crowd, the widow's family, and the prophet. You are Finances for the visions you impart into Your children. You are the Parting of the Red Sea and the Miracles of Christ. You are the Channel through which people are led from captivity to liberation. You are in the midst of all impossibilities. You said, "Everything is possible for him who believes." You are who You said You are. You are the Bishop and Chief Shepherd of my soul. Your law is the apple of my eye. You are the Soon-Coming King.

You are El Shaddai, the almighty God. You are Everything to me. You are Jehovah Nissi, the Lord my Banner of Victory. You liberate me from the strongholds of the enemy. You are the Lord my Righteousness. You release me from shame and guilt, my God. You restore what the enemy has stolen from me. You are Jehovah Jireh, my Provider. You are Finances to me, for You became poor so that I can have a full supply. You are the Lord my Sanctifier. You break me free from the clutches of this world. My God, You are Everything to me. You are All-Sufficient. I do not need You plus anything. You alone are More Than Enough. You are More Than Enough!

You are my Wisdom. Father, I believe the wisdom You have given to me surpasses the natural appearance of my circumstances. Your action plan infuses me with faith to step beyond the natural limitations of human rationale. I know I have enough faith because, God, You said You have given to me "the measure of faith." I can act on my faith to see Your kingdom come and Your will done in the physical arena. I can soar in Your divine ability in the middle of an impossible situation because, God, You are the Highway of Deliverance right where I am. You are to me whatever I need today.

Oh, God, You said You will go before me, and Your glory will be my rear guard. A thousand may fall at my side and ten thousand at my right hand, but, You said, terror, pestilence, and destruction will not come near me. Hallelujah! You will watch over me.

Father, You said, "I will hasten my word to perform it." You watch over Your Word, so when I step out in faith on it, You do it. God, You are not a liar. You will do what You say because You are committed to Your Word and You love me. Thank You for being who You said You are. Hallelujah! I Am is with me! God, since You are for me, who can be against me? In Jesus' name, Amen.[12]

---

12. See Appendix B for Scriptures upon which this prayer is based.

CHAPTER FIVE

SENSORY REACTIONS OF FEAR

The third cause of fear God revealed to me is the reaction of our five senses to natural information. You see, our senses can induce great fear as we process negative natural information. We saw in the previous chapter that information itself can result in fear because it has a powerful voice. But, if we do not know how to silence our strong negative reactions, runaway emotions can control our lives. God wants to enable you to rule your emotions despite your sensory reactions.

Our Senses React to Personal Experiences

Biologically, when a stimulus engages any of our senses—sight, hearing, smell, taste, or touch—they react. When one or more of them react to something, it can affect us emotionally, creating fear and inhibitions. Because we are human, every one of us experiences sensory responses. Our senses continually react to natural information, and we often anticipate the worst. If our senses react with doubt or uncertainty, we can become fearful.

Unfortunately, most of us have not considered why we experience fears that arise from our senses. In any situation in which your senses react or receive information, you must consider how pessimistic your thoughts and expectations are about what you encounter. In this chapter, we will examine the extreme conclusions you can draw from your senses. Exaggerated or false and baseless conclusions often result. Remember that when false evidence, showing itself as being real (F.E.A.R.), affects our senses, it induces fear.

Do you expect the worst?

For instance, if you wake up in the middle of the night and smell smoke, what happens? Does instant panic and fear hit? Are you convinced your house is burning down? Or if you hear a siren close to your home, do you immediately think a family member has been in an accident? When you look at your checkbook or credit card bill, does fear grip you? If you eat something that tastes odd, do you instantly suspect food poisoning?

When you have a deep cough, do you assume you have pneumonia? When you suffer from a headache, do you conclude it must be an aneurysm? If your heart palpitates or you have indigestion, do you panic, thinking it is clearly a heart attack? If you feel a small lump under your skin, are you convinced it is the initial stages of cancer, from which your great-grandmother died?

If you receive a letter from the Internal Revenue Service, do you assume it must be notice of an audit, a massive levy, or a penalty?

Are you continually affected negatively by what you see, hear, smell, taste, or feel? Do you dread certain sights, sounds, smells, tastes, or touches? When your senses repeatedly react in this manner, your life is riddled with tension. Whatever you encounter, you conclude that the worst-possible scenario is unfolding. If this describes your life, you are living in bondage to fear. Each time you envision the worst because your senses react spontaneously to natural information, fear is the driving force. Your sensory reactions are inducing fear and limiting you.

A clear example of this is the story of "Beth and Todd" that I told you about in Chapter One. Although I changed the names to protect the privacy of the individuals involved, their story is true. A close male relative sexually molested this young woman when she was just a small child and then again when she became a teenager. Without realizing it, she developed a fear of all men.

Despite the defenses that she built around her, though, this young woman fell in love with a Christian man whom she met when she went away to college. He loved her from the start, but proved himself to her over the years. When he asked her to marry him, she wanted to say yes and trust that God would help her handle the physical intimacy of marriage. Now, let me share the rest of their story.

She did marry him, trusting that God would heal her. However, even though both of them were Christians, fear still held the young woman in captivity. Whenever her husband lovingly caressed her, she relived the lustful touch of her relative in that dark basement. The devil used her senses to invoke fear. Although she knew that her husband loved her and that he would never do anything to harm her, she still could not get beyond the terrible memories that his touch invoked.

This would be a tragic story if that were how it ended. But God is stronger than our experiences of the past. His love and power silenced the voice of this woman's senses. Eventually, through the patient love of her husband, the healing truth of the Word of God, and the transforming power of the Holy Spirit, a miracle took place. God healed this woman and set her free from fear. Now, many years later, she is still happily married to that same man, and she faithfully serves the Lord who set her free from her prison of fear.

Do you see how our senses can limit us and bring us into great bondage? However, God can and will deliver us!

Our Senses React to News Media and Other Sources

Not only must we contend with our sensory reactions to our personal experiences, but we also must deal with our reactions to what we see or hear happening to others. As we discussed earlier, most of the free world has instant access to nearly an infinite amount of information through radio, television, newspapers, and the Internet. Add to this messages we can receive via E-mail, cellular phones, pagers, and fax machines, and we can become inundated with incessant information. Unfortunately, much of this is bad news. We can sit in our living rooms and witness horrible events as they unfold thousands of miles away. These sights and sounds can instill great fear.

Ground Zero—I Was There

Where were you on Tuesday morning, September 11, 2001, when the hijacking terrorists attacked the United States? At that time, I was with my son, Eric, in a tunnel in New York City's train system. We were in mid Manhattan about twenty to thirty blocks from what would soon become Ground Zero in lower Manhattan.

Just five minutes before the first hijacked plane, American Airlines Flight 11, crashed into the north tower of the World Trade Center, Eric looked out the train's window at the Twin Towers. The buildings were in perfect shape. It was a typical day in New York as the train took us underground.

Little did we know what would happen next. By the time our train returned to the street level at Madison Square Gardens, chaos had completely engulfed the city. What had happened while we had been underground?

Eric and I jumped into a taxicab. Soon, we learned that our driver had been parked in front of the World Trade Center as the first plane hit the center's north tower. In a state of shock, he immediately had sped away and parked on the side of the street, where we entered his cab. Dazed, the driver now made no sense as we asked what was happening. He turned the radio up as loudly as possible and screamed, "Look around behind you!"

Eric and I turned to see huge plumes of smoke billowing from the burning World Trade Center! The south Twin Tower had vanished, leaving a gaping hole in the skyline next to the smoking north tower!

Reality hit us as the authorities moved to close off Manhattan, trapping us on the island. All around us, a myriad of people streamed down Wall Street and fled north through Central Park into upper Manhattan, hoping to exit through the northern sectors. However, with no way of escape, we all were forced to spend the night on the island. Because I knew one of the managers, Eric and I were able to stay in a hotel. That night, though, across the entire city, thousands of people literally slept on the streets because they could find nowhere else to stay. Hotels opened their ballrooms and other areas for people to sleep on the floor since this nightmare now trapped everyone there.

Shortly after the attack, my wife, Faye, called my cell phone. Watching a television in Delaware, her reaction to the horrible events was much greater than mine, although I was right there in Manhattan! She saw and heard the most dramatic, detailed pictures and sounds the media could capture, while Eric and I simply saw a plume of smoke above other buildings and people rushing to leave the island. My son and I did not see the airplanes crash or the firemen and police rush into the towers just before the buildings collapsed.

> Merely seeing a tragedy broadcast live can have great negative effects.

The war-zone carnage was not continually paraded before our eyes as it was for those watching their televisions. Because the media constantly bombarded its audience with the sights, sounds, and information from the attack, Faye had a greater reaction to it at a distance of more than 100 miles away than we had in being there. Think about this. We often do not realize how powerful the communication age really is. The pictures we see and the sounds we hear through the media influence us more than we recognize.

Faye became a little frustrated with me as we talked over the cell phone. She wondered why I was not reacting as she was.

"They have shut off the island," Faye informed me.

"Well, okay. We'll get a hotel room," I replied.

"No," she explained, "they're not letting anybody in the hotels."

"I know somebody up here who can get us in. Don't worry, Faye."

As we talked, I watched a sea of people coming up from southern Manhattan. However, Faye experienced something dramatically different as she stared at the television. She kept seeing over and over and over and over again the airplanes crashing, the rescue workers rushing into the buildings, the towers collapsing, and the ashen people frantically running away. Faye kept hearing replays of the terrified people screaming and the startled news reporters explaining the horrific events as they unfolded.

"Eric and I will get a hotel room," I told Faye, "and we'll get something to eat."

"Are you going to eat?" Faye asked, at first in disbelief. Then she quickly added, "Get three days of food."

I meant we would go out to dinner. I thought, *Man, that's a big dinner!*

No, Faye wanted me to get a supply of food and water to last several days because, from what she saw and heard, it appeared that all facilities in the area were completely destroyed. We were communicating on two different levels because we were not seeing and hearing the same things.

I had planned to go to an auction in New York that evening, so Faye asked, "You're not still going to that auction tonight, are you?"

"Yes, Faye, I'm going."

She immediately replied, "No, Gary, don't go. I want you to say this, 'I will not go.' Tell me you won't go, Gary!"

"Faye, I can't say that." I was still planning to go.

"You're going to say that!" she insisted. "Don't you know what you're facing?" Faye was frantic. To relieve her, I eventually agreed not to go to the auction.

Quickly I realized the reality of the events had not impacted Eric and me in Manhattan nearly as much as they had Faye in Delaware. It was all because of the television media. When Faye and other people watched the news, they worried for us more than Eric and I feared for ourselves. I am not making light of the events in any way. I simply mean that the television pictures and sounds more powerfully impacted people at a distance than the reality of the situation affected us, who were physically just blocks away from Ground Zero at the time.

Eric and I knew we were in a serious situation when we saw more than a hundred thousand panicked people rushing toward us to get off the island. However, a great disparity existed between this sight and what Faye saw. The pictures and sounds she received from the television had a paralyzing effect. However, because we did not see them, we escaped much of the fear Faye and others felt.

Repetition Has a Powerful Impact

Why were Faye's and my responses so different on September 11, 2001? Through our senses, we both experienced the attack, but our reactions differed greatly. The reason is that when believers or unbelievers sit in front of televisions to see the same negative pictures and hear the same negative rhetoric over and over and over again, they begin to meditate on it and continually rehearse it. The same happens whether our eyes and ears react to a horrible event replayed on television, we read something bad over and over again, or we hear negative information told to us continually. The repetition causes it to have an increasingly deeper grip on our lives. Our senses react, and we can become paralyzed with fear, unable to take the correct steps.

> Keep God as your primary Source of information—not the media.

We must stop this fear-peddling frenzy, which has produced a stronghold not only in our nation and much of the world but also in the church. It is debilitating the church, causing us to be inactive and ineffective in bringing deliverance to the world. The same frightening pictures and doom-filled messages that bind them also bind many of us.

What can we do to combat this problem? Do we simply tune out information as if it does not exist? No, we must be aware of the facts, but we had better understand spiritual realities and God's nature so we can live successfully in the midst of conflicts and challenges. We need to live not by the reaction of our senses but by God's Word.

We must, as we discussed earlier, avoid overindulging in the wrong source of information, which caused the first instance of fear in the garden of Eden. Keeping God as our Source of information is essential instead of focusing on the devil's constant display of evil, especially through the secular media. Remember, our enemy uses the media to saturate us with fear-inducing information. A constant feeding on this bad news without God's Good News is very detrimental to our spiritual, physical, and mental health.

We need to evaluate how much time we spend watching, reading, or hearing the news. For example, if we spend twenty hours a week absorbing the news and worldly programming, how can one forty-five-minute sermon on Sunday undo the impact of those twenty hours of negative messages?

A War for Our Beliefs

Rehearsing constant negative information causes fear to grip us, torment to hold us captive, and confusion to cloud our judgment. These effects steal our time and abort the purposes for which God placed us on this earth. We are at war today. This is a war not only against unseen physical enemies, but also with another unseen enemy. This one is spiritual. He works to overthrow our very faith in God's truths and His authority, as well as God's nature that resides within us. We are in a war for what we believe.

Carl von Clausewitz (1780–1831),[13] the Prussian army officer, military strategist, and definitive expert on Western war, defined *war* in a very interesting way. In his classic treatise *On War*, he wrote: "War…is an act of violence intended to compel our opponent to fulfill our will."[14]

Read that definition again. Physical and visual terrorism and crime are forms of war. Crime and terrorism produce what? Fear. Many criminals and terrorists perpetrate violence with the intention of causing us to fulfill their wills of succumbing first to fear, then to their beliefs, political policies, or ways of life.

Have you noticed that most of the news headlines and reports produce fear? Then what will you receive from watching, listening to, and reading the news for hours? You will experience great fear. Now, I am not saying the media is intentionally terrorizing us, but the devil uses this natural information to arouse our senses to fear. He is at war for our beliefs, thoughts, and emotions, and he will use whatever means is available to try to destroy us.

You must recognize that the purpose of gripping negative news from the media and other channels is not simply intended to disturb your day. Its purpose is to dominate you and to bring you under the subjection of another's will: the devil's! Are you ready to recognize that you have been the devil's target to bring you to absolute fear? This is not a single act but a continual flow before your eyes and ears to turn your beliefs and life from God. This is the devil's war against us.

---

13. "Carl von Clausewitz." Encyclopaedia Britannica, 2002. <http://www.britannica.com> (27 May 2002).

14. Carl von Clausewitz, *On War*. Ed. Anatol Rapoport (Vom Kriege, 1832; Trans. Routledge & Kegan Paul, 1908; London: Penguin Books, 1968, 1982), p. 101.

The Bible explains this war:

For though we walk in the flesh, we do not war according to the flesh. For the weapons of our warfare are not carnal but mighty in God for pulling down strongholds, casting down arguments and every high thing that exalts itself against the knowledge of God, bringing every thought into captivity to the obedience of Christ. (2 Corinthians 10:3–5)

Let's read this passage in the *New International Version:*

For though we live in the world, we do not wage war as the world does. The weapons we fight with are not the weapons of the world. On the contrary, they have divine power to demolish strongholds. We demolish arguments and every pretension that sets itself up against the knowledge of God, and we take captive every thought to make it obedient to Christ. (verses 3–5 NIV)

Here we see that our war is to keep ourselves focused on the knowledge of God, maintaining Him as our Source of information. The enemy will attempt to establish strongholds in our lives to cause us to wallow in ungodly mental pictures, arguments, and pretenses. However, we must keep our beliefs and thoughts aligned with Christ. This is the war we face, but we have mighty, divinely powerful weapons to fight it!

Repetitive Thoughts Cause Further Harm

If we are not vigilant in battle, we may suffer seriously. As a consequence of being inundated with reports of horrible events, people are not sleeping at night. They are having difficulties walking in peace. Fear and worry grip them. They are confused. People are jumping to wrong conclusions. They are experiencing psychosomatic illnesses. Great challenges are arising in many people's lives.

When constant negative information indoctrinates people, it is very easy to turn them in its direction. In fact, it is almost child's play to

> We assist the enemy when we saturate our minds with fearful thoughts.

dominate or manipulate people who have been filled with bad news. In this way, some people have given themselves over to human and spiritual enemies and do not know how to become free. They have lost the battle and have subjected themselves to the will of another.

This does not necessarily mean their enemies are inflicting additional harm. Some of these victims are creating their own challenges by saturating themselves with a constant barrage of media reports and pictures. If they continue in this cycle and do not break it, they can become mentally and spiritually paralyzed, numb, and unable to carry out their purposes. They can even become terminally ill.

It's Time to Take Back Your Senses!

God's Word speaks peace to troubled hearts.

Today, we must make some sobering decisions. With unwavering authority, we must refuse to be puppets in the hands of the liberal, trained editorialists. We must not succumb to those who create a fearful environment through sensationalism, using the principle, *If it bleeds, it leads.* Do you want to live under their constant grip on your mind? God has wisdom for you to live in peace even in the midst of perilous times, and it does not come from watching the secular media. It comes from God's Word. This is the only way to overcome your sensory reactions.

In the Old Testament, the Israelites created small containers, known as frontlets, which contained tiny scrolls of passages from God's Word. They tied these on their foreheads and arms, so they would continually have the Word of God before their eyes. As Christians, we do not literally wear the Word of God, but we look to Jesus, *the* Word of God. The book of Hebrews instructs:

> *Looking unto Jesus the author and finisher of our faith; who for the joy that was set before him endured the cross, despising the shame, and is set down at the right hand of the throne of God. For consider him that endured such contradiction of sinners against himself, lest ye be wearied and faint in your minds.* (Hebrews 12:2–3 KJV)

Here we see that we are to fix our eyes on Jesus. What will happen if we don't? We will become wearied and faint in our minds. You see, if we do not saturate ourselves with the Word, we can very easily lose our focus and run off course. Our minds, and therefore our lives, can run amuck. We will be ruled by our senses.

We Are Powder Kegs

It is time to realize that for the past forty years, we have been set up. We have bought into ever-progressing sensationalism, perversion, and distortion of truth. We have spent money going to movies and hours watching television screens. By doing this, we have spent much of our lives envisioning other people's terror, fear, destruction, confusion, and disorientation. After years of this building up, we have become like powder kegs set to blow. The news of one terrible event can light the fuse, and our lives can come crashing down around us, paralyzing us in fear. Why? Because we have been predisposed to believe the worst. This is a war, and all it takes to capture us is one negative report. That's all!

As believers in God, we should not live this way. Do you realize that believers are preset to believe God, not the worst? When we accepted Christ as our Savior, the Spirit of God came to dwell in us, connecting us to Him. He and His Word became preeminent in our lives. We received the measure of faith to believe God over anything else. Now, if you have spent your life positioned in front of constant death, destruction, and other ungodly things that Hollywood has produced and the media has reported, you have predisposed yourself to believe the worst instead of God's best.

To illustrate this, compare the number of hours you have spent throughout your life watching and listening to movies and other forms of media versus the amount of time you have spent in God's Word, training and developing yourself in His perspectives. Which category has more hours? If you are like most people, Hollywood and the media win by far, not the Word of God.

This must change. We cannot fulfill the purposes God has designed for us if we constantly drown out His voice from our lives. God and His Word must be our highest priority, constantly before our eyes and ears and stored in our minds and hearts.

It's Time to Break the Cycle

This challenge is not new. The Israelites in the Old Testament had to learn how to undo years of negativity before they could move into the Promised Land. Let's look to the book of Joshua to see how God told them to accomplish this change. This example clearly illustrates the process of returning your priorities to God's Word.

Earlier, we discussed how the Israelites came under the new leadership of Joshua when Moses was about to die. Remember, the children of Israel had been through forty years in the wilderness. The previous generation had died because they were at odds with God and refused to trust Him. They had murmured, were negative, became afraid, and constantly complained against Him, His provisions, and His servant Moses. Because of this, remember, God had vowed to give the Promised Land to the *second* generation instead of to the negative first generation of parents.

> **Meditating on God's Word can remove the devil's negative influence.**

This was the atmosphere in which Joshua grew up. He lived in a backslidden nation, filled with negativity. After the sinful parents had all died, God spoke to Joshua, the new leader of Israel, saying,

> *Be strong and of good courage, for to this people you shall divide as an inheritance the land which I swore to their fathers to give them. Only be strong and very courageous, that you may observe to do according to all the law which Moses My servant commanded you; do not turn from it to the right hand or to the left, that you may prosper wherever you go. This Book of the Law shall not depart from your mouth, but you shall meditate in it day and night, that you may observe to do according to all that is written in it. For then you will make your way prosperous, and then you will have good success. Have I not commanded you? Be strong and of good courage; do not be afraid, nor be dismayed, for the LORD your God is with you wherever you go.* (Joshua 1:6–9)

In the above passage, God promised Joshua that He would be with him. For a moment, think about the war we are in. Remember, whatever we need

God to be, He is that to us. We must fear not, for I Am is with us and is greater than whatever we fear.

This is wonderful news, but how can we get rid of the fear we naturally feel? God gave Joshua the answer: *"Meditate in it day and night"* (verse 8). This means to mutter and speak His Word over and over again. Why was Joshua to do this? It was so he would *"be careful to do everything written in it"* (verse 8 niv). Joshua needed the Word ever pres-ent in his hearing, in his mouth, and before his eyes, so it would constantly release faith within his heart. This is the only way he would prosper and succeed in God's purpose for his life and for the people of Israel.

It is critical to understand why this was important in Joshua's life. Remember, for forty years he had lived surrounded by a people of negativity. Joshua needed the negative effects of forty years removed in a very short time, so he could step into and seize what God had promised him.

Likewise, we live with very similar circumstances. As a nation, we have had about forty years now of constant inundation of other people's misery from an instrument that has captured our lives: television. If we are to possess the promises of God, we must unshackle ourselves from the past forty years of negativity and turn to meditating in God's Word. This is how we will win the war for our beliefs. We must regain the ground we should not have lost.

Today, let's break the cycle of feeding on negative information. Let's reverse the effects of countless hours of seeing, hearing, and speaking the world's information. Are you ready to wage war on fear, torment, confusion, and disorientation? I believe this is your day of breakthrough. You do not need to live in bondage anymore. No longer must you be a casualty of war, subject to another person's will. You can become free as countless others have!

> Rehearse what God has already done for you.

David Moved Beyond the Natural Plane

The Bible contains many examples of people breaking through their sensory reactions and fears to freedom. Only then could they fulfill God's purposes in their lives. Earlier, we discussed the account of David facing Goliath.

It is a clear example of this principle. Remember, when the men of Israel looked at the armored giant, Goliath, and heard him taunting them and their God, they all fell into fear. Their senses reacted and induced fear. Then David came along. He did not share the rest of Israel's fear because, instead of hearing the enemy rehearse all the horrible things he planned to do to the Israelites, David rehearsed all the supernatural feats God had done in his life. David recalled how God had provided the strength for him to kill a bear and a lion with his hands when they stole his father's sheep! Goliath would be no different.

Do you see the difference in focus between David and the armies of Israel? The armies rehearsed the negative news and threats, while David rehearsed the positive results of trusting in God. Despite impossible odds, David *knew* God would be with him when he fought Goliath. He relied upon the great I Am to be with him as promised.

Young David convinced King Saul that he could fight the giant and win, so Saul agreed. However, Saul first suited up David in his armor, trusting it would protect the lad against Goliath. A natural, carnal man, Saul believed that without his own armor, David did not stand a chance. Saul told David, *"You are not able to go out against this Philistine and fight him; you are only a boy, and he has been a fighting man from his youth"* (1 Samuel 17:33 NIV). Saul insisted that David had to use these natural weapons in order to have a chance at defeating the giant.

Before he went into battle, David clumsily clunked around in Saul's armor to see how it felt. I will paraphrase the story here. Uncomfortable in the armor, David declared, "This is miserable stuff. I have to get rid of it. I have not proven this armor. I don't know if it works, but I *do* know what works: God. Let me go with God and take what I have in my hand, my slingshot. I'll just grab a handful of stones and be on my way. I don't need anything else. My confidence is in my God. I Am is with me. He's all I need."

> Victors live on a supernatural plane.

You see, David and Saul operated on two different planes of sight. Saul lived on the natural, carnal level, in which his senses reacted and his emotions ruled. He walked by the appearances of what he saw, and by what he heard, smelled, tasted, and touched. David, on the other hand, lived in the supernatural arena with his focus on God. He refused to allow natural tactics to dominate his senses or rule his emotions. This is why David did not fall into fear. Because he chose not to limit himself to his sensory reactions, David became free to move in a dimension beyond his natural senses. He operated in God's supernatural strength to kill the giant enemy.

You can defeat your giants, too, if you do not allow fear to bind you. Remember, fear is a spirit of bondage. It will limit you, causing you to feel as though you live in a straitjacket, rendering you powerless. God has a better way.

Only Two Spies Rehearsed the Good News

The book of Numbers records a conflict among men whose senses ruled them and others who were not sense-dominated. Here twelve Israelites witnessed a natural situation. All except two responded according to their senses. Let's read this account in which the Lord instructed Moses to send twelve leaders of Israel to scout out Canaan, the land God had promised to them. Pay close attention. You might have heard this story before, but if you do not live in the victory of it, you have not heard it in your spirit.

Bringing back a huge cluster of grapes and other fruit from the Promised Land, the twelve men reported to Moses after their forty-day exploration. They said,

We went to the land where you sent us. It truly flows with milk and honey, and this is its fruit. Nevertheless the people who dwell in the land are strong; the cities are fortified and very large; moreover we saw the descendants of Anak there. The Amalekites dwell in the land of the South; the Hittites, the Jebusites, and the Amorites dwell in the mountains; and the Canaanites dwell by the sea and along the banks of the Jordan.

(Numbers 13:27–29)

The men observed a well-fortified land with large cities where powerful giants lived. In spite of the fruits they had carried back, the messengers were reluctant to possess and occupy Canaan because they could not get past

> Focus on God— not on the obstacles in your way.

the dangers they had seen. Instead of focusing on God and His promises, they focused on the apparent obstacles that were ahead. They relied on their senses and fell into fear.

However, not all the twelve spies reacted this way. Two, Joshua and Caleb, saw the same situation differently. Now, this was forty years before Joshua became the new leader of Israel. "*Then Caleb quieted the people before Moses, and said, 'Let us go up at once and take possession, for we are well able to overcome it'*" (verse 30). We will read in a moment that Joshua agreed with Caleb. Only Joshua and Caleb returned, saying, "We are well able to possess the land." All the rest said, "We are not able."

> *But the men who had gone up with him [Caleb] said, "We are not able to go up against the people, for they are stronger than we." And they gave the children of Israel a bad report of the land which they had spied out, saying, "The land through which we have gone as spies is a land that devours its inhabitants, and all the people whom we saw in it are men of great stature."* (Numbers 13:31–32)

It is interesting to note that, in Hebrew, the phrase "*bad report*" means "defaming, evil report, infamy, slander."[15] With these reports, the men literally defamed and slandered the Promised Land, which upset God![16]

If allowed, fear can silence faith.

Numbers 13:33 continues their evil report: "*There we saw the giants (the descendants of Anak came from the giants); and we were like grasshoppers in our own sight, and so we were in their sight.*" This verse says, "*We saw….*" They had seen the giants with their own eyes. Their senses screamed that the giants were huge, and they reacted accordingly. Therefore, the giants became a BIG problem to them.

Do you know some "big-problem people"? Everything is a big problem for them, even when God promises otherwise! I have seen a truck driving around our city. It has a bumper sticker that says, "If the job's too big, your god's too small." I like that. Nothing is too big for *my* God! How about yours?

---

15. *Strong's Hebrew and Greek Dictionaries*, H1681.
16. See Numbers 14:36–37.

What else did these ten spies see? They said, "*We were like grasshoppers in our own sight, and so we were in their sight*" (Numbers 13:33). Their senses reacted to natural information, and they fell into fear instead of believing God was with them. In doing this, they questioned God's omnipotence. They discounted His ability to sustain them in battle against the giants and saw themselves as mere grasshoppers.

Numbers 14 records that an intense atmosphere of fear reigned over Israel after the ten spies brought back these terrifying tales of Canaan. This commotion caused Joshua and Caleb to warn the Israelites against the fear of doubting God's protective power. They exhorted Israel, reaffirming God's ability to subdue their enemies so they could possess the land. Then Joshua and Caleb pleaded with the people: "*Only do not rebel against the LORD, nor fear the people of the land, for they are our bread; their protection has departed from them, and the LORD is with us. Do not fear them*" (Numbers 14:9).

Fear dominated all but two of the Israelite spies, whom Moses had sent to investigate the Promised Land. However, it was too late, because those who believed they were not able to possess it had already had their voice. I call them the "not ables." They turned all of Israel to fear, despite the faith-filled testimony of Joshua and Caleb, the "ables."

> How big is your God?

This fearful report incurred God's wrath. He condemned the cynics among them to a life of affliction and death in the desert, saying: "*But as for you, your carcasses shall fall in this wilderness*" (verse 32). Then God killed the ten sense-dominated spies with a plague. However, Joshua and Caleb lived and eventually inherited God's promises. Joshua went on to lead the children of Israel into the Promised Land forty years later. You see, fear insults God by questioning His infinite ability and faithfulness to His promises. It belittles Him and can provoke His anger.

Gnosticism Rears Its Ugly Head

Like Gnostics, as we discussed earlier, who combine God with other instruments of success, the Israelites did not trust God. They placed Him second as they sought other avenues of success. Thinking they needed God plus provision, they refused to trust in Him alone. They failed to accept that *"man shall not live by bread alone; but...by every word that proceeds from the mouth of the LORD"* (Deuteronomy 8:3). They needed to learn it is not God plus provision. He *is* Provision. Consequently, God made them wander in the wilderness for forty years, where they died, not experiencing the fulfillment of His promises in their lives. Instead, their children inherited their promises.

Unfortunately, we are not much different. As I mentioned before, many Christians have also adopted a form of Gnosticism. We think we need more than God. We need more than His Word, more than what He says. We need God plus our senses satisfied, God plus an avenue to believe. We look for other roads to success, and then add God to the equation. Think about it. Have you ever thought you needed God plus something? Be honest. If so, you have bought into a snakelike mentality, which has separated and detached you from the true, living God. This is the God who said, *"I am watching to see that my word is fulfilled"* (Jeremiah 1:12 NIV). What God has said, He will perform. You do not need anything but this.

If you find your senses looking for something else to meet your challenge, or if you are searching for a natural solution, stop right there. Realize that God, who has spoken to you—whether personally (*rhema* in Greek) or through His written Word (*logos* in Greek)—is able to do what He promised. End your search now, and turn to Him only. With Him, you are well able to possess your Promised Land!

The "Not Ables" Outnumber the "Ables"

Today, we still live in an environment of "not ables." Do you know some "not ables"? They try to get you to live under the response of their senses. Unfortunately, not many see life as God promised. A great majority see life as it feels, living under the responses of senses. I thank God, however, that the "not ables" do not rule His kingdom. The body of Christ operates with the "ables" giving ability to the "not ables." The "ables" live in His revelation, and the rest benefit from them.

> The "ables" live in God's promises.

I know very few "ables," so I make sure to stay in touch with them all. You should too. Let that sink into your spirit. I have a list of "ables," and when I am ready to run with a vision, I call them. I share with them my dreams. Each time, their only concern is, "Did God talk to you?"

"Yes," I answer, "God said to do this."

"Then we're able," they always answer. "That's all we need: 'God said.' Let's do it! Hallelujah!"

They never tell me, "Don't do it." They never complain, "It's going to take a miracle for that to happen." They never, ever ask, "What do you have to make this happen?" No, if God said it, that settles it for them. I like to be around "ables."

To Receive God's Promises, Do Not Listen to Your Senses

You must understand this about God: You will never receive what He has for you if you listen to your senses. They have no ability to bring you into His promises. If you believe your senses, you will fall into fear, which will enslave you until you break it. When you live in the shadows of fear, it will control you until your senses disengage from the misrepresentation of natural information.

When God, who is the End from the Beginning, tells you something, don't look at the odds according to your senses, then say, "God, I can't do it." He knew your obstacles before He gave the promise to you! Don't you think He planned to deal with them *before* He directed you? Do you think when you discovered your obstacles, it was a shock to God? No! I have never read in the Bible that God ever said, "Oh, Holy Spirit, what are we going to do about this problem?"

Yes, I know that your senses can become very riled. Your feelings are constantly screaming, but don't listen to them. Don't let them impair you. We all face this challenge from time to time, even some of us who have had direct encounters with God speaking and giving visions to us. We still confront and even fall victim to this kind of fear, in which our senses react to natural information. However, we must rise above the noise of our screaming senses.

We must shut down the voices of our natural insights—perceptions, feelings, physical sight, hearing, sense of smell, taste, and touch. In the next several pages, we will discuss how to do this, but before we do, declare this now:

> God, what You speak to me is true. I rebuke my senses, which debilitate me, causing me to doubt You and bow in fear. Fear, you must bow to me because I am one of the "ables" in Jesus' name. I will run with God's vision, despite all odds against me.

My Senses Scream

I have practiced what I am preaching here. Believe me, I understand how hard it is to shut off the voices of the senses. Every week, my senses scream regarding what God has promised me, but I do not listen to them anymore! Let me share some of my experiences.

In 1975, when God called me into the ministry, my wife, Faye, and I were headed for divorce. I knew that for me to be in the ministry, my home had to be in order. Fear tried to grip me because being separated from my wife, who hated me, was not exactly having my house in order! My senses screamed that I could not work for God in this condition.

God instructed me to love Faye as we went through this great trial.

I said, "God, it hurts to love that woman."

"You have to learn to love other people," God replied, "so start with your wife!"

"But," I complained, "this one hurts because she's living with my best friend!"

God's answer was not what I wanted to hear: "Baby-sit your children for her," He said, "so she can have her freedom with him."

What! My senses rebelled. My feelings ripped through my gut. The pain I would face in obeying the Lord was more than I could bear. My senses felt as though they were short-circuiting. I could not fathom even being nice to Faye and my former best friend, much less *baby-sitting* for them! What was God thinking?

"God," I finally said, "something has to happen inside me here because what I'm feeling is not exactly cooperating with what You're saying!" Fear gripped me because my ministry seemed to be at stake also.

"If you learn to love her," He quietly promised, "you can have her back."

"Oh, God, now *that's* a promise I can stand on!" All it took was that one promise from God to sustain me.

I began to baby-sit my children in obedience to the Lord. Many times I was in the living room with them, while Faye and my best friend went back to the bedroom! I did not like it. My senses screamed. I could barely contain myself to sit there without breaking down their door. However, I knew I could not listen to my senses. No matter how difficult it was or how long it took, I vowed not to react according to my natural instincts. I knew that my senses had no ability to get God's promise for me. I had to be dead to them. This was the only way I would receive God's promise of bringing Faye back to me, so we could pursue the life that God purposed for us!

> Obedience to God brings blessings.

I chose not to allow my senses to dictate my choices, as I declared, "God, what You said is more valuable than what I feel about it." I refused to allow my feelings to obstruct God's plan for my life. It eventually worked just as He had said it would. I began to love Faye as I had never loved her before, despite our separation and her continuing affairs. She was with one, then another, and another.

Then one day Faye demanded, "Gary, I want a divorce, but I can't afford it."

God immediately said to me, "Give her everything she wants."

"Are You saying, God," I asked Him, "that you want me to give Faye the divorce and pay for it?"

"Do it," He said.

Oh, but I loved her and did not want the divorce. By this point, God had done a miracle in my life. I was not bitter. No longer did pain plague my heart. I had no ax to grind with Faye. I loved her and knew what God had spoken! I knew she was to be in the ministry with me, so a divorce would take me further from God's dream for us. Yet, because God said it, I obediently paid for the divorce. My senses did not enjoy writing the check, but I financed the divorce and gave Faye everything she asked for.

The day we divorced, however, I asked Faye to go on a date with me. Since we both now were single, I took her to lunch! I continued to love Faye and obey God, trusting He would turn her heart back to me and we would be in ministry together.

It all paid off because God did bring Faye back! After we divorced in 1976, we remarried each other later that same year, and we have stayed married ever since. Now, we minister together for the glory of God. *Charisma & Christian Life* magazine published this as their cover story in February 1991. Also, you can read more about it in my upcoming book, *It Only Takes One.*

Your Emotions May Not Support Your Dreams

Many people look for emotional support for their dreams. However, when their emotions seem to contradict their dreams, they fall into fear. You must remember that emotions cannot support fearlessness. Only God can. When God gives a dream to you, it does not matter if your emotions counteract it. You see, by obeying God despite your feelings, the proper emotions come and your dream manifests! That's how it works.

My wife and I see this in many marriages. Because of our powerful testimony, we often minister to married couples. We frequently hear them complain that because they do not love each other anymore, they want to divorce. Many couples claim they married for love and will stay married *only* if they love their spouses. Once they lose love, they fear they cannot gain it back. This is a wrong mind-set. The feelings of love may not last forever, but our commitments to our mates must. There is no guarantee that you will always have the right emotions to solve your marriage challenges. However, you will always have the Healer of Marriages—God! If you are not in love with your spouse, you can mend your broken marriage by committing to obey God and staying together. The feelings of love will return as you obey Him.

I remember when Faye and I went through our divorce, she blatantly told me, "I'm not in love with you anymore, Gary."

"Well, that's no secret," I said. "I'm not in love with you either." I think this shocked her because I was refusing to accept divorce. I had repeatedly told her of my desire to continue our marriage.

"Don't you love me anymore?" Faye asked me, probably wondering why my words now seemed to contradict what I had said earlier.

"Yes, I do love you," I explained, "but I'm not 'in love with you.' You do some stinking stuff that I don't like," I honestly continued, "but I love you, Faye."

Bewildered, she asked, "What does *that* mean?"

"It means I'm willing to sacrifice everything to see you restored," I explained. "I'm willing to continue seeing you. I'm willing to give my all to make our marriage work. It's because I love you, Faye, not because I feel great about you right now."

Eventually, God gave love to me for my wife. Now, I am so much in love with Faye that I can hardly contain it all. However, love came only after my decision to obey God. It came after my commitment and sacrifice. It came in spite of my emotions.

Breakthroughs Cannot Come from Feelings

It is critical to remember that you will not receive your breakthroughs when you entertain your feelings. If you trust what you feel and sense, you will not go beyond what you feel and sense. You will never experience God's promises if you continue to allow your senses to speak too loudly. The resulting fear will crush your dreams.

You might feel rejected at some point when you resist the control of your feelings. Jesus did, too. Men rejected, ostracized, scorned, struck, afflicted, and crucified Him, but Jesus did not yield to His human feelings. The Bible says of Him:

He is despised and rejected by men, a Man of sorrows and acquainted with grief. And we hid, as it were, our faces from Him; He was despised, and we did not esteem Him. Surely He has borne our griefs and carried our sorrows; yet we esteemed Him stricken, smitten by God, and afflicted. But He was wounded for our transgressions, He was bruised for our iniquities; the chastisement for our peace was upon Him, and by His stripes we are healed. (Isaiah 53:3–5)

For we have not an high priest [Jesus] which cannot be touched with the feeling of our infirmities [or "weaknesses," NIV]; but was in all points tempted like as we are, yet without sin. Let us therefore come boldly unto the throne of grace, that we may obtain mercy, and find grace to help in time of need. (Hebrews 4:15–16 KJV)

Your pain, feelings of infirmities, weaknesses, and fears touch Jesus because He experienced these same emotions and temptations when He walked on the earth. However, He did not succumb to them. Take your feelings to Jesus, and He will become the Healer of your "feeler." The Spirit of Grace will help you overcome them.

> **Jesus is the Healer of your "feeler."**

When you begin to feel your negative emotions taking charge, recognize what is happening. Seek the Lord's help. Run to Him when you sense hurt, despair, animosity, hopelessness, anger, and any other conflicting emotion. As you have read, I dealt with a lot of fear from the hurt when I was going through marriage problems and divorce. Nothing hurt more than that. However, because I conquered that hurt, I now know how to avoid living by feelings. Nothing has or will ever rule me by hurt again because I have decided to obey God with my emotions. In Him I decreed that hurt would never have me in its grip again. Thus, my life has become a testimony to God's ability to rescue His children from their runaway emotions.

He will do the same for you! Do not anticipate the "inevitable" next hurt to come your way, so you can add it to your list of reasons why you cannot move forward. Instead, decide that hurt or the fear of hurt will no longer control you, in Jesus' name!

Break through Cancer!

No matter what your obstacle is, God has a way for you to break through to His promise for you. Ignore your senses, and receive your miracle in Jesus' name. Even if your obstacle is that dreaded word *cancer*, God is your Healer! Even if the doctors have pronounced a death sentence over you or your loved one, God is your Healer! Even if no one on earth has any hope for you or your loved one, God is your Healer!

I remember hearing John Osteen[17] tell the healing testimony of his wife, Dodie. In 1981, she had terminal metastatic cancer of the liver. The doctors gave up all hope for her survival, but God supernaturally healed her! This was in 1981, and she is still in remission. Dodie went on to write a book, *Healed of Cancer.*

John talked about one Scripture verse that especially helped Dodie and him through the struggle they had with fear of the cancer. At that time, I did not comprehend much of what he said. However, as I heard the story over and over, my spirit grabbed hold of it, and I finally understood. As I recall, Dodie had cancer in her back, lungs, and throughout her body. She was very, very sick. John said he continually read Isaiah 41:10 as he walked around their house with Dodie. Together, they meditated on this powerful verse. Remember, we read it earlier: *"Fear not, for I am with you; be not dismayed, for I am your God. I will strengthen you, Yes, I will help you, I will uphold you with My righteous right hand."*

John said they walked around with this prognosis of death on Dodie, and they declared, "Fear not, for the I Am is with thee." They continued meditating on and quoting Isaiah 41:10 day in and day out. They knew they could not give in to their senses.

John said not only was cancer destroying Dodie, but fear was strangling them both. Their fear was giving the cancer license to kill her! Think about how much fear can grab hold of you with the diagnosis of cancer. To defeat the cancer, they had to break that fear first. One of the ways they did this was by

> Meditating on God's Word makes fear bow.

---

17. Pastor John Osteen (1921–1999) founded the Lakewood Church in Houston, Texas. For further information about this church and its continuing ministry, visit their website at www.lakewood.cc.

meditating on and confessing this Scripture in Jesus' name. Then God completely healed Dodie Osteen. Hallelujah! That was more than twenty years ago.

Meditate on God's Word

As John Osteen told the story of Dodie's healing, he talked about the benefits of meditating on God's Word. Remember, earlier in this chapter, we read how God instructed Joshua to meditate on and speak forth His Word day and night:

> *This Book of the Law shall not depart from your mouth, but you shall meditate in it day and night, that you may observe to do according to all that is written in it. For then you will make your way prosperous, and then you will have good success.* (Joshua 1:8)

Remember, Joshua needed to meditate on God's Word to remove the previous forty years of fear and negativity. John and Dodie Osteen had to do this as well. We all must do it.

When John described Dodie's healing, he explained how meditation works. He said that when we meditate on a portion of God's Word, the passage is like stones in a brook on top of a mountain. The stones tumble downstream, eventually all the way to the ocean. Have you ever seen a streambed where it empties into the ocean? The stones from the stream are smooth and clear. Some are even translucent. Likewise, as we read, speak, and meditate on a Bible passage, it rolls over and over in our spirits like the stone rolling downstream. Eventually, it becomes pure and crystal clear. Then we can see deep inside that passage. This is what happens when we meditate on God's Word. It becomes crystal clear with nothing to block our insight of it.

Isaiah 41:10 Is for You, Too

When God said in Isaiah 41:10 that He is with you, will help you, and will uphold you with the right hand of His righteousness, He was telling you that the victory is because I Am is with you. He perpetually declares to you,

"Fear not." Why? It is because the God who is well able is standing there to remove the fear. He is bringing to you deliverance, freedom, preservation, healing, wholeness, and a bright future because of who He is. It is not because of a methodology, principle, or law. It is because the living, abiding person of God Himself is present to help you in your conflicts and challenges.

Declare:

God, You said to fear not because You are with me, so I fear not! I fear not! I fear not! Fear not! Fear not! Fear not! Fear not! Fear not! Fear not! Fear not! Fear not! Fear not! Fear not! Fear not! Fear not! Fear not! Fear not! Fear not! Fear not! Fear not! Fear not! In Jesus' name, I said, "Fear not!" Fear not! The more times I hear it, the less I fear!

As we discussed in an earlier chapter, meditating on and speaking Isaiah 41:10 has helped me immensely. If you apply it to your life, it will do the same for you. In fact, right now, I encourage you to meditate on it. Declare it aloud, regardless of what your senses tell you about your circumstances: *"Fear not, for I am with you. Be not dismayed, for I am your God. I will strengthen you. Yes, I will help you. I will uphold you with My righteous right hand"* (emphasis added). Say it again.

Now, put your name in it:

(Your name), don't fear. I Am is with me. (Your name), don't be discouraged. I Am is my God. I Am will strengthen me. Yes, I Am will help me. I Am will uphold me with His righteous right hand. So, (Your name), don't ever fear. The great I Am is with me.

Even after you repeat these words only a couple of times, you will sense a change in the atmosphere. Why? At the beginning of this declaration, you talked for several sentences about your emotions and how they work. Then you brought in the I Am and unleashed the great ability of God's presence. His anointing itself breaks yokes of bondage, including the bondage of fear:

And it shall come to pass in that day, that his burden shall be taken away from off thy shoulder, and his yoke from off thy neck, and the yoke shall be destroyed because of the anointing. (Isaiah 10:27 KJV)

Don't underestimate the power of meditating on God's Word! You simply *must* do it. There are no shortcuts.

Open-Heart Surgery Prevented!

Several years ago, doctors discovered that one of the ladies in our church had some blocked arteries. She underwent an angioplasty, a medical procedure to unclog blood vessels with a balloon-tipped catheter. The doctors had said that if this procedure was unsuccessful, the woman would need open-heart surgery. Unfortunately, the angioplasty did not work, so the surgeons planned to do a coronary bypass.

> **Fear can block God's promise of healing.**

Fear gripped the woman. Her senses screamed at the natural reports she heard. She had several blocked arteries. The first procedure did not work, and now the doctors wanted to go back in to do open-heart surgery. This had the woman's attention. She knew she had to break the fear that paralyzed her, or she would not receive God's promise of healing. The woman decided to trust God and not her senses.

Before she went into the hospital the second time, she was anointed with oil, according to the Bible:

And they [the disciples] *cast out many devils, and anointed with oil many that were sick, and healed them.* (Mark 6:13 KJV)

Is anyone among you sick? Let him call for the elders of the church, and let them pray over him, anointing him with oil in the name of the Lord. And the prayer of faith will save the sick, and the Lord will raise him up. And if he has committed sins, he will be forgiven. (James 5:14–15)

She also studied and meditated on Scriptures about not fearing. She continued this until she broke through the fear and understood I Am was with her!

Before the bypass surgery, the doctors checked the woman's heart to pinpoint the locations of the blocked arteries. When they did, they found absolutely nothing wrong! All the blockages were gone. The woman's cardiovascular system was completely open. She was healed! Her doctors were amazed at the miracle.

What would happen if *you* could make fear bow and unleash the presence of God in *your* life? What if *you* could rise above your sensory reactions? What if *you* could stop trusting in natural information and break its effect on your life, so you could connect to the ability of God? If you could do this, then God's creative wisdom, ability, and anointing would flow. Suddenly, your challenge would be over. It would be history. You would be free. Would you like that? You *can* have it. As you have seen throughout the previous pages, this has already happened for countless people of God, such as David, Joshua and Caleb, Dodie Osteen, the lady with the heart condition in our church, my wife Faye, and me. *You* can be next!

Touch Jesus Now

Are you ready for a change? If so, it will cost you. Remember, it cost Jesus His life to free you. Do you know what one of your costs will be? You need to exercise your hand by picking up the remote control for your television and clicking the power switch off! You *do* know that you have authority and control over it, don't you? The television does not *have* to be on most of the time. As you turn it off, declare to God:

Father, You said You will hold me by Your right hand. I am ready. I am turning off the world's source of information to free myself for You to be my Source of information. Hallelujah! I will look to You and Your Word for my Source.

Now, call on Jesus to touch you. Open your spirit to Him. Give your feelings of past hardships to Him. If you have felt that people blocked you, held you down, or hurt you, it is time for you to put those feelings into the hands of God. Let the Spirit of Grace have your feelings. In fact, let Him have the people who hurt you. Let Him have your spouse, brother-in-law, sister, father, mother, former pastor,

> Give your hurts to Jesus.

and current pastor. Whoever has hurt you, give them to God to deal with as He sees fit. Then, if your feelings have affected you, pray this now:

> Father, You know my heart. You know my life. You know where I have been. You know what has happened to me. You know what I have faced. You know what I have done and said. You know my failures. You have seen my fears. You know what I have felt. You know what I have allowed to rule me. God, no one on this earth knows me as You do. You know my thoughts before I think. You know the number of hairs on my head. There is nothing unknown to You.
>
> God, You also know the dreams and visions You have given to me. You know what You have spoken to me, Father, and I know what You have promised to me. You said I can be free of the effects of my feelings. You said Jesus can be touched with the feeling of my infirmities because He was tempted as I am, yet without sin.
>
> Jesus, You can sense and experience what I feel. Right now, I give my feelings to You, so You can become the Healer of my "feeler." Spirit of Grace, help me to overcome my feelings of fear that have come from what I have seen, heard, smelled, tasted, and touched. Father, I ask for Your anointing to break the yokes from my life. Holy Spirit, my Helper, come to my aid. In Jesus' name!

Do you have a few feelings that you do not want to keep? Are you ready to die to them? If so, confess this aloud:

God's Holy Word declares that the weapons of my warfare are not carnal, but they are mighty through God to pull down strongholds. Right now, I speak to the effects of hurt and pain in my life. I declare that I am dead to them. Senses, I am dead to you because the Word of God declares:

> *For ye are dead, and your life is hid with Christ in God.*
>
> (Colossians 3:3 KJV)

> *For if we have been united together in the likeness of His death, certainly we also shall be in the likeness of His resurrection.* (Romans 6:5)

I have been crucified with Christ; it is no longer I who live, but Christ lives in me; and the life which I now live in the flesh I live by faith in the Son of God, who loved me and gave Himself for me. (Galaitans 2:20)

Since I am dead in Christ, I am free of the effects of my feelings. Every demonic feeling of disappointment, hurt, failure, and fear must bow to Jesus. Every cause that has made me feel "not able" must bow to the Word of God, which says I am well able.

Take a moment to picture the battle you are in now. Pray once again:

Father, my spirit knows the great I Am is with me. I will not be discouraged. I Am is my help. Yes, I Am strengthens me and upholds me with the right hand of His righteousness. I Am is with me. Therefore, I break the power of fear. In Jesus' name, Amen.

CHAPTER SIX

ENTERTAINING EVIL IMAGERY

Many of us live with secret, fearful imaginations. When we are gripped by troubling or enticing images, we usually do not realize that the spirit of fear is attacking us. Instead, we simply put up with these thoughts, believing they are part of our humanity. However, this is not true. Demonic spirits can implant fearful imagery in our minds, and we must eradicate it! It can appear falsely pleasant or alarmingly scary, but either way, it results in fear and bondage.

Do you realize that the only way to become free of your darkest mental images is to expose them? The enemy does not want you to know this truth! Perhaps you have lived most of your life trying to hide these secret imaginations. That's what the devil wants you to do. Maybe you have never trusted anyone to open the doors of these haunting pictures and voices that have entrapped you. The thought of exposing them can be very scary. That's how Satan keeps you bound. However, I assure you, this is the way to find peace and freedom from evil imagery.

Today, through this book, I am asking you to allow me access into this fourth area that causes fear. Are you willing to uncover these pictures and images that no one has ever known about before? It will require honesty on your part and the understanding of how this demonic deception operates. I will share this life-changing knowledge with you. Then, if you can be honest, I believe within the next several moments you will break a barrier of hidden imagery and fear. This will allow you to live freer than you have ever thought possible!

Imagine how it would be to live in freedom and peace. You *can* live this way. In fact, it's only a few pages away! Truly, it can be that simple, because the power of God is in these words. He loves you and wants to set you free today. Come with me now into the inner recesses of your heart and mind. What do you have to lose except fear, pain, bondage, and destruction?

What Is the Picture in Your Mind?

What images fill your mind?

Most communication operates in mental pictures, not necessarily in words alone. Satan is very skilled at using imagery to trick us. In this chapter, we will discuss how he and his demons attempt to steer us off course by implanting false impressions in our thoughts, so that we will lose perspective of God's desires and life's fulfillment. Here we will explore how to defeat our enemy and restore God's faith-empowered imagery in our hearts.

We have all seen pictures painted on the canvas of our minds. You see, when we drive down the road, read books and magazines, watch television and movies, use our computers, enter different environments, fall asleep, or awaken, we pick up images in our minds. These pictures can be alluring or frightening, and they can come from demonic spirits. As though they were real, these scenarios often play out in our minds with us or our loved ones in them. Fear results. Many of us do not know how to break their effects before they literally start to guide, dominate, and possibly even control us.

Often, the enemy's imagery occurs when we encounter certain environments. For instance, when you find yourself in high places, you might imagine yourself falling to your death; or when you drive across a big bridge, you picture your car veering off the edge, plunging into the water. Perhaps when you walk into a hot, stuffy room, you have the impression that you are suffocating or choking. Maybe when you visit a very sick person or simply drive by a hospital, you picture yourself dying of a horrible disease.

Maybe bad dreams have haunted you. Often when children go to bed at night, they imagine ghosts or monsters attacking them in the darkness as a result of movies they have seen. The enemy is responsible for planting such portraits of disaster and evil in our minds.

Since these images are not real, many try to dismiss them as though they cannot hurt us. However, Satan is the source of these pictures. Remember, in Chapter Two, we discussed the effects of relating to the wrong source of information. If we do not keep God as our Source of information, we invite disaster into our lives. Trouble comes when we begin to embrace imageries from the devil.

> The devil's evil images can become our reality.

For example, you may sit down to pay your bills and immediately begin to worry that you will be unable to meet your financial responsibilities. You imagine having to sell your house. Then you see your car being repossessed. Soon you begin to believe that you are doomed because that frightening scenario projects you in living-color failure. You envision yourself painted into that picture of inadequacy as it plays in a continuous loop in your mind. Before long, that negative image becomes even more real to you than the literal facts of your circumstances.

The enemy also brings up pictures of true events of failure from your past. With these, he creates new images of failure in your future. You imagine that yesterday's defeats will repeat themselves. Have the pictures in your mind painted you into a program of future failure? Can you see very plainly that you will not succeed in particular plans? These types of images paralyze many of us.

Some people fear marrying again after a divorce, for example, because they continually see in their minds the images of their former broken homes. This happened to Faye when I proposed to her again after we had divorced each other in 1976. The thought of remarrying the same man she had recently divorced was scary, especially because I was the man! Images of our former horrible lives together haunted her. Just before we were to remarry, Faye felt as though she were standing on the edge of a cliff, with God asking her to jump. She had to believe that He was really there and would put our marriage back together.

Faye knew Jesus' words concerning marriage: *"Therefore what God has joined together, let not man separate"* (Mark 10:9). However, trusting that God would be with her at that time and in that circumstance was difficult. The fear of failure worried her as she pictured us going through another divorce. Yet, despite the fearful images in her mind, Faye obeyed the Lord, and I am very happy she did! To date, we have been married more than thirty years—with nine months off for bad behavior, as I like to say!

You must realize and learn to recognize quickly that when your mind's imagery is pessimistic, it is not rooted in God's plan for you. If you see images of yourself failing or faltering in something that God has promised to you, this imagery is not from the Spirit of God. Remember, we read in the previous chapter that those who follow God are "ables." If you see images of yourself as "not able," it is from the pit of hell! This imagery is designed to debilitate you. I love to take the enemy's false images that come into my mind and compare them with this promise from God: *"'For I know the plans I have for you,' declares the LORD, 'plans to prosper you and not to harm you, plans to give you hope and a future'"* (Jeremiah 29:11 NIV).

All images that do not agree with these plans from God are from the enemy; therefore, I reject them.

Satan Counterfeits God

Before we move into victory, we must answer some questions. Where did all this imagery originate? Why are we susceptible to the devil's images? Satan does not originate anything new but counterfeits the principles of God.[18] He merely steals and distorts God's plans to advance his own misleading, seductive schemes. You see, the Spirit of God is the original Image Maker. The Holy Spirit communicates with us through impressions in our spirits. He conveys images of His messages to us. Then, to lead us off track, the devil tries the same method.

In the book of Genesis we find God, the Image Maker, at work before man ever existed. When God created the heavens and earth, the Holy Spirit moved over the face of the earth in the chaotic darkness. He started to envision the image of other creations. Let's read the account:

---

18. See 2 Thessalonians 2:3–10.

In the beginning God (prepared, formed, fashioned, and) created the heavens and the earth. The earth was without form and an empty waste, and darkness was upon the face of the very great deep. The Spirit of God was moving (hovering, brooding) over the face of the waters. And God said, Let there be light; and there was light.   (Genesis 1:1–3 AMP)

The Holy Spirit was like a mother hen, brooding over her eggs before hatching her young. Being an Image Maker, He constructed *images* of light and other creations before actually creating them. The Spirit formed the images before the "hatching" took place. Then, through His spoken Word, He created the world.

God later made man in His own image:

Then God said, "Let Us make man in Our image, according to Our likeness; let them have dominion over the fish of the sea, over the birds of the air, and over the cattle, over all the earth and over every creeping thing that creeps on the earth." So God created man in His own image; in the image of God He created him; male and female He created them.   (verses 26–27)

Nowhere in the Bible does it say any of God's creation is in His image— except man. We know the devil wants to defeat God. Since man alone bears God's image, it is easy to see why Satan desires to destroy us. He wants to annihilate the image of God in the earth. Consequently, we have become his targets. One of the devil's greatest tools is to turn our focus from the Image Maker to the image counterfeiter. Satan does this by conjuring up his fear-producing, debilitating images in our minds, trying to short-circuit the pictures God shows to us regarding our purposes.

> We were created in the image of God, the Image Maker.

The devil also can tempt us to entertain images of suicide as a way to destroy us and abort God's purposes. Satan can make suicide appear as a good way to escape our problems, but it is a false sense of freedom. One man I know recently shared that he was on the brink of suicide. The picture continually played in his mind that there was no way out of his financial problem. As a possible answer, the imagery of his death filled his mind. He saw the insurance company paying off his debt, his wife marrying a "better" man, and his children being "better off." Yes, his death seemed to be the only answer! I thank God, however, we reached this man before his imagery became that family's nightmarish reality.

This imagery was a lie from the pit of hell. God did not want that man to die. He has a purpose and a plan of financial deliverance. One inspired idea from God could set this man free. Remember, trusting God is the answer. Suicide is *never* the solution. It is *always* against God's will because He is the Life-Giver.

God's Pictures of Purpose and Promise

When the Spirit of God speaks to me, I see images of His communications. Do you? I see what the message entails, its effects, and its ramifications. This is how God conveys His purposes to us. He speaks to us with images. As Habakkuk said, "*I will…watch to see what He* [God] *will say to me*" (Habakkuk 2:1). Similarly, we often ask one another today, "Do you see what I am saying?"

An example of the Spirit speaking in a vision occurred to me in 1975. During a time of fellowship in the Spirit, I remember God showed me an image of fields of people. He said, "You will lead these by the tens of millions to Me." Then I watched as the fields of people came to Christ. Trusting in God's promise, I recognized that the Holy Spirit would bring to my remembrance what Jesus had said to me. He planted this imagery in my spirit, and I replayed it often in my mind afterward.

The natural information around me screamed that this vision from God could never happen. This is when my wife and I divorced. The devil tried to replace God's imagery in my mind with his own disheartening pictures of my failure. I remember saying, "Dear God, You have one big mess here." Yet, despite the rough times, I clung to God's imagery because I knew it was an impression regarding His purpose for my life. Now, I am seeing the manifestation of this vision. Hallelujah!

> Satan tries to cover over the images God has implanted within us.

Do you have impressions from God that came early in your walk with Him? Are they still resident in the back of your mind and heart somewhere? When God inscribes His images in you, they become part of your being. Satan may have tried to implant His images in you to block out God's impressions of His promises. However, I believe that if you will pull away the satanic clutter, you will rediscover that the Holy Spirit's images have not dissipated.

I encourage you not to miss God's images communicated to you. Do not permit Satan's imagery to overwhelm your God-inspired visions. If you do, debilitating fear will result. Always remember, Satan designs pictures in your mind to abort God's purposes and promises. It is important to separate images the devil instills from those of the Holy Spirit.

In our Bible school, the School of Biblical Studies, we teach about imagery in great detail. We discuss how Satan counterfeits God through imagery in our minds with the goal of taking us off course in life. If we focus on demonic impressions, we will lose perspective of God's purposes and promises. We cover all this in the course *Victory in Spiritual Warfare.*[19]

How Satan's Enticing Imagery Works

Chambers of Imagery in the Old Testament

Remember, we discussed in the last chapter that we are in a war for our beliefs. The reason Satan constructs images to dominate our minds is so that he can eventually control our beliefs. If we permit this, we will digress from God's will.

We have studied how the devil uses frightening pictures this way. Now let's examine how he tries to control us with images of temptation. The book of Ezekiel shows how Satan utilizes compelling, enticing imagery to pervert God's purpose for His people and to steal their worship.

In chapter 23, Ezekiel told a parable of two promiscuous sisters, Oholah and Oholibah, who entertained images of filth and deception. They became captivated by the images of handsome Babylonian officers and Assyrian

---

19. You may order the course separately or enroll in the Bible School, which is located on campuses around the world and in a home-study format. For more information, contact our ministry or visit our web site, www.gwwm.com.

governors, commanders, and warriors. Their sensual imagery consumed these two harlots, and they chose to live out these imageries by prostituting themselves. Ezekiel explained:

> Her sister Oholibah saw this, yet in her lust and prostitution she was more depraved than her sister. She too lusted after the Assyrians—governors and commanders, warriors in full dress, mounted horsemen, all handsome young men. I saw that she too defiled herself; both of them went the same way. But she carried her prostitution still further. She saw men portrayed on a wall, figures of Chaldeans portrayed in red, with belts around their waists and flowing turbans on their heads; all of them looked like Babylonian chariot officers, natives of Chaldea. As soon as she saw them, she lusted after them and sent messengers to them in Chaldea. Then the Babylonians came to her, to the bed of love, and in their lust they defiled her.   (Ezekiel 23:11–17 NIV)

The images of fulfillment, which these two sisters pursued, culminated in their destruction. They began to worship the idols of the men they lusted after. Consequently, their lifestyles alienated them from God and eventually ended in their untimely deaths. They became victims of satanic imagery. Read the entire chapter to understand how alluring satanic imagery distorts and destroys God's purpose for His children's lives.

As a prophet, Ezekiel often received supernatural insights through encounters with God. On one such occasion, the Lord unfolded how in darkness the Israelites were walking in demonic imagery. Ezekiel saw in the Spirit that they were physically worshipping false idols and pictures, secretly following their misguided imaginations, which their enemy had inspired. God supernaturally showed their "chambers of imagery" to Ezekiel. Let's read about it.

> Then said he [God] unto me [Ezekiel], Son of man, hast thou seen what the ancients of the house of Israel do in the dark, every man in the chambers of his imagery? for they say, The LORD seeth us not; the LORD hath forsaken the earth.   (Ezekiel 8:12 KJV)

Here the Israelites became susceptible to the devil's lies by permitting his images to seize control of their lives. This subsequently drowned out God's vision of victory. They became blind to God's encouraging images of promise and fell into idolatry and destruction.

Chambers of Imagery Today

Above, we saw how Satan's beguiling pictures plagued the thoughts of the two sisters and the Israelites, causing them to succumb to idol worship. The same process operates in our lives today. We conceive tempting images in our minds, worship them by continually entertaining thoughts of them, and then eventually may commit these acts of sin. However, regardless of whether we *physically fulfill* our sinful thoughts, simply *entertaining them in our minds* is sin! Thus, we fulfill the devil's dream of defeating God's purposes for our lives.

Jesus clearly revealed that sinning with only our minds is not innocent fantasy but is actual sin:

> *You have heard that it was said to those of old, "You shall not commit adultery." But I say to you that whoever looks at a woman to lust for her has already committed adultery with her in his heart. If your right eye causes you to sin, pluck it out and cast it from you; for it is more profitable for you that one of your members perish, than for your whole body to be cast into hell.* (Matthew 5:27–29)

Demonic spirits are at work in every area of our lives, producing volumes of sinful imagery in the chambers of our minds. They cause you to see enticing, imaginary scenarios of yourself. These pictures can be so vivid and real that you can practically smell, taste, and even touch them. They speak to you, making you feel as though you are actually there, living the pictures.

Such imagery may look, feel, and seem pleasurable, but it is truly deceptive and destructive. It can easily become your secret retreat, which you habitually desire to visit. This secret life can become an escape from your real life. When this happens, you defeat God's purpose for your very existence on the earth today because He has plans that you are missing.

> Fostering a "secret life" keeps you from fulfilling your God-given purpose.

For example, let's examine how this works in a marriage. God has designed marriage to be a gratifying and enjoyable experience between a man and a woman. However, we can easily abort this plan. Here's how it often occurs. The husband sees a pornographic image on the Internet or in a magazine, closes his eyes, and visualizes having sex with another woman. When this happens, the devil has infiltrated the chamber of this man's imagery.

Or the wife reads a lewd romance novel, then pictures someone other than her husband in bed with her. She has given the chamber of her imagery over to the devil. This also can happen outside marriage. For example, a single person goes to bed at night and invites erotic images to provide consolation for a restless night. Alone in the dark, he or she may choose to return to those images night after night. A demonic spirit is controlling this person's chamber of imagery.

Consider another example. Let's say someone has greatly wronged you. Instead of settling the matter biblically, you begin to hate this enemy with a passion. To console yourself, you evoke violent, bloodthirsty thoughts against the person. You imagine stabbing, shooting, or in some way inflicting harm. Dwelling on these demonic pictures confirms that Satan dominates your chamber of imagery.

Some of the most destructive forces surface in the mind as alluring and savory images. These include the brief sense of victory that comes from imaginary vengeance, the superficial joy of abusing drugs and alcohol, and the illusion of power that results from committing rape or murder. The devil nurtures in man's mind deadly, deceptive images of fulfillment such as these, trying to exert control. In doing this, he entices man to fall prey to his lies.

When we adopt patterns of escapism and fantasy, we tune out God. We focus on our imaginary lives of imagery and falsehood. These demonic images lure us away from God's blessings and direction. Our lives become farces, and we leave no room for God's purposes.

Also, when we harbor demonic images, it often is an indication that we are failing to trust wholly in God and refusing to seek His solutions to our challenges. In our desperate attempts to find relief in difficult circumstances, we rely on a false sense of comfort that demonic images offer. This, however, creates fear because we are not following God. Subsequently, another fear can afflict us, the fear of having personal secrets exposed. In addition, guilt and shame frequently replace the false picture of satisfaction and achievement that comes from indulging in demonic imagery.

Pictures the devil instills in the mind always are sources of snowballing destruction. This is his hidden agenda. He will hold captive the chambers of our imagery until we release ourselves from his grip by submitting to Christ's divine intervention. Later, we will discuss this process in detail, but remember this promise from the Bible: "*Submit yourselves therefore to God. Resist the devil, and he will flee from you*" (James 4:7 KJV). Our minds can become free of demonic imagery because we have the right to "*have the mind of Christ*" (1 Corinthians 2:16 KJV).

> The devil's pleasurable images soon prove to be prison bars.

Your Dark "Little Secret"

If you are engaging in private, demonic imagery, it can become your dark "little secret." When this happens, the devil gladly waits for the opportunity to expose it to other people. In this way, your hidden secret becomes the enemy's stronghold on your life. He creates devastating images to illustrate the potential consequences of the discovery of your secret. Then the devil paints you into these horrifying pictures. To protect yourself, you keep your private thoughts tucked away and hope no one will discover them.

If you allow the devil to haunt and torment you this way, it will create fear. You will envision failing in the future because of these pictures. You will doubt your ability to prosper. The threat of guilt and pain, resulting from exposure, will be your constant companion. Eventually fear will paralyze you, and your secret will become your private corner of hell.

Eradicate the Imagery of the Enemy

Uncover Your Secret

Do you have a "skeleton in *your* closet" that could destroy your future? If so, why don't you publish it in a book or share it with others? I am serious!

That's what I did. I wrote my story in my book *Conquering Your Unseen Enemies*. If you will expose your secret, you will no longer live in fear of being caught—because you have nothing to hide. Telling everyone you are a sinner breaks the enemy's stronghold on your life. It's time to eradicate the effects of demonic imagery. Uncovering your secret is the answer!

I have done this, and now I live in "a glass house." My life is a public record, open and visible for all to see. If you research the name Whetstone at the library of the University of Delaware, you can read about my life. It is public knowledge. I have no secrets. Since becoming a Christian, I have openly repented of everything in my life that I know of to uncover. If I find more, believe me, I will let it out because I know that what I hold in secret has the power to snare me.

Sometimes my history comes to visit me at Victory Christian Fellowship, the church I pastor. However, everyone there knows about my negative history, so it is no longer a threat to me. My past cannot hurt me now because it has become my Christian testimony! If someone wants to bring it up, it only brings glory to God because He rescued and transformed my life. I find it very interesting that the devil doesn't bring up my past very often anymore!

Yes, I know we all fear being honest and open, and we don't want anyone to know our secrets. However, we must expose our indulgence in the enemy's imagery. The cost of keeping it hidden is too great. We must open our secret sins and deal with them. That's the only way to stop being a victim of satanic imagery.

Be Freed from the Restraints of Past Failures

Let me share a specific example from my life. I once was afraid of achieving a high level of effectiveness in leadership. The cause of my fear was an image of a past failure, which the devil continually tormented me with in my mind. You see, before I became a pastor, my wife and I had owned several businesses, which had grown to ten million dollars per year in sales. However, when we came to a certain threshold of revenue, our business started falling apart organizationally and structurally. I

> God will transform your past into a testimony of His grace.

did not know how to advance beyond this level. We had three retail stores, a large wholesale company, a manufacturer's representative firm, and a small-business consulting company. Some said I was simply spreading myself too thin. However, I knew a lack of knowledge was my challenge.

Several years later, after I became a pastor, the devil tried to haunt me with that business failure when similar circumstances emerged. In the church, as I led my administrative team, relational (not economic) challenges started to develop. As in our business, I came to a point in the ministry at which I felt I had gone far enough. It appeared I had depleted the resources necessary to take me higher in God's work. I felt constricted.

Immediately, I thought, *I've been here before. I've seen this in my business. I don't know if I can break through this, because I did not do it before.* The devil talked to me through this negative image. Have you ever "been here before," seeing the same picture of yourself where you were when you failed? When this happens, the details are very clear. The image the devil had firmly sown in me assured me of certain failure again, and I became the victim of fear.

However, instead of retaining these private accusations in my mind and allowing them to stifle me, I opened my heart to our congregation. I explained exactly what I was going through, calling on the church to pray for me. I was not afraid of what anyone thought or said. It did not matter whether my confession would shock people, or if it would lead to love or hatred for me. I simply wanted out of my chamber of imagery. I wanted to break the effect of this tormenting hellhole, in which the devil had pegged me with the same failure. I did not want to live there again. I needed victory. I refused to be afraid of anyone, because the Bible says, *"The fear of man brings a snare, but whoever trusts in the* Lord *shall be safe"* (Proverbs 29:25). You see, if we worry about what others think, we cannot become free of fear.

In this situation, I could not afford to mistrust anyone because I desperately needed freedom. My entire ministry depended upon it. I had to overcome the fear of mistrust by trusting God and everyone around me. Yes, I might have had "a Judas" as my friend. Jesus did. However, even in the presence of a Judas, the Lord promises safety and freedom. I had to trust Him. He was my only hope of escape. Through the prayers of my church, I was able to rise above this imagery to walk in God's promises.

Today, as a pastor to many pastors, I often see that the fear of confessing their own faults binds many pastors. Once, when I ministered at a pastors' conference, the Lord revealed to me that this is one of the greatest challenges for pastors. By never confessing their faults to one another, they set themselves up to fall. As I began to share this insight with the pastors, the auditorium became very quiet. "We are about to have an altar call before other brothers' hearts," I explained. Then the Lord led me to instruct the pastors to reveal to their brothers in Christ, other pastors there, the areas of their greatest torments. We shut off the television cameras, turned off the recorders, and had church for about three hours. Many pastors openly confessed and dealt with their faults to become free. Hallelujah! We had a tremendous time of victory in the Lord.

> Confession is a step toward freedom.

Recognize the Power of Porn

Last year, I received a special-delivery letter marked "Personal and Confidential. For Dr. Whetstone's Eyes Only!" What I read inside shocked me beyond belief. Here's the story.

The letter was a plea from a board member of a Christian denomination in the U.S.A. The request was simple: He was asking that I refer to their ministry headquarters any Bible school graduates I considered morally upright, in good standing in the community, and proficient in preaching and teaching. Since our ministry includes the School of Biblical Studies, which has trained thousands of pastors and lay ministers, this was a reasonable request.

However, the reason was greatly disturbing. "We are short-handed in our pulpits," the letter read, "due to the immense number of our pastors who are in a time of restoration resulting from pornography." Yes, pornography was the problem! Secretly, day after day, these men had been snared in the ever-present web of porn that is available and pushed upon everyone who uses the Internet. The results were devastating. Some were getting divorced. Others were turning to homosexuality, perversion, and other snares.

Satan's den of imagery is at our fingertips: *on the Internet*! Absolutely, no one is exempt from the enemy's evil imagery. We *all* must be on guard. If you have become involved in pornography, get ready to be set free!

Regardless of the kind of evil imagery—pornography or anything else—that may torment you, it is time to uncover your struggle. Let it out. If kept hidden, your secret has the power to destroy you. However, if you uncover it, you open the doors to repentance and a new beginning with God. The sins resulting from demonic imagery need not keep you in secret bondage any longer.

> Replace Satan's images of misery with God's visions of hope.

They can serve as a testimony of repentance, the devil's defeat, and victory in God. Always remember, until your sin has become your testimony, you will experience even greater temptation!

Right now, you can become free. In the following sections through the end of this chapter, I will explain specifically how to do this. After you finish these sections, you need to deal effectively with your secret. Although you may not trust another human being on the face of the earth at this level right now, you need to start. Ask God to help you find a Christian who will support your decision to become free of the evil imagery and who will hold you accountable. Confess and uncover your burden, get rid of it, and end its power over your life forever.

Invite God into the Chambers of Your Imagery

Are you ready to break the devil's power over your life right now? Are you sure? To eradicate the imagery will cost you, but it is well worth the price. Once you bring light to the darkness and break through its imprisoning walls, you cannot secretly return to your hiding place. You will be free, never to live in that dark cell again. Its influence of destruction and failure will be gone!

To clean the chambers of your imagery, you must trust God implicitly. Let Him have your greatest secrets and fears. He knows you. He knows where the devil has bound you. Trust Him with your inadequacies and your life. Trust Him with the images that cause you to escape His mandate or excuse yourself.

Pray to God, opening up and confessing your past, your secrets, and your fears. Submit to Jesus' healing power. His blood will cleanse you, set you free from your secrets, and release you from your fears. You can make your fears bow to Him! Then invite God to intervene in the chambers of your imagery with pictures that portray His promises. Pray this now:

Father, I reaffirm my faith in You, Your Word, and Your promise to fulfill what You said. I look to You and seek the fullness of Your power in my life.

Right now, I open myself to You, Father. I trust You with my inadequacies and my life. I confess my secrets, Lord. I submit the imagery of my mind to You and repent of my attraction to Satan's false imagery. Oh, God, my involvement in this sinful practice has opened the door to fears and secrets that have bound me and caused me to miss Your will. I do not want the enemy to trick and limit me anymore. No longer do I want to escape my life, but I desire to live for You, Father, from this day forth. I rededicate my life to You, Lord. Help me to be good soil upon which the seed of Your Word will bear fruit.

Today, I turn from Satan as my source of information to You. Father, forgive me. Jesus, cleanse me with Your blood. Set me free from my secrets and the bondage to fear. Loose me from the chains in my life. Help me to overcome all barriers regarding drugs, finances, relationships, jobs, marriage, sexual perversion, anger, and everything else the enemy has tried to bind me with.

I call on You, Holy Spirit, my Helper, to replace the devil's imageries that have snared me and pictured me in the imagery of failure. I ask You, Spirit of God, to bring into my life renewed images of the Lord's deliverance and hope. I believe that You will perform a miracle in my life and redirect me in the path of righteousness. Help me to walk in Your ways from this day forth, so I may fulfill Your purpose for my life.

Thank You, Jesus, for washing me with Your blood, so I can come to our Father's throne this day. You are worthy. You are worthy. I give to You all the praise, glory, and honor for this testimony of deliverance from Satan's imagery in my life! Hallelujah! In Jesus' name, Amen.

Cast down Evil Imagery

Remember, the Bible declares:

For though we walk in the flesh, we do not war according to the flesh. For the weapons of our warfare are not carnal but mighty in God for pulling down strongholds, casting down arguments ["imaginations," KJV] and every high thing that exalts itself against the knowledge of God, bringing every thought into captivity to the obedience of Christ. (2 Corinthians 10:3–5)

If you want to remove all the demonic imaginations, strongholds, and ungodly high things in your life, you must use your spiritual weapons to pull them down. Then think thoughts of obedience to Christ. I encourage you now to speak boldly to the demonic images that have caused you to mistrust God's infinite ability and fall into fear. Now, pray and bind these images in Jesus' name:

> I declare the Word of God will destroy the chambers of evil imagery in my life. I rebuke all demonic images of fear, in Jesus' name. I rebuke the pictures in my mind that have tried to make me feel inadequate and unqualified for God's grace and promise. I bind you in the name of Jesus. I speak to the tormenting pictures the devil has given to me: You will no longer bind me. YOU are bound! Loose my body and mind in Jesus name!
>
> Fears, release me now. I refuse to cower in fear any longer. You will not cripple me in my flesh today, condemn me for my past, or cause my former failures to be repeated in my future. I speak to those demonic images: Go from me in the name of Jesus. I speak to the fear of man: Go, in Jesus' name.
>
> I speak to every sense of guilt and shame: Go, in Jesus' name. You have no power over my life, for Jesus bore my guilt and shame. I will not live with you anymore. I am free from all demonic strongholds in Jesus' name!

Shout to the Lord! You are free of these satanic imageries in Jesus' name!

Replace Demonic Works with God's Revelation

Now, it is critical for you to develop an intimate relationship with God so that you can easily distinguish between the devil's images and those of the Holy Spirit. You do not want to fall into this trap again. If, in the future, you become tempted to entertain demonic imageries and fantasies again, grab your Bible and fill your chamber of imagery with God's Word! Meditate on it daily to keep your mind free of satanic clutter and filled with God's promises and purposes and obedience to Him. This is how you can walk continuously in your newfound freedom, which Jesus purchased for you! Hallelujah! This is very important. Jesus warned us of the consequences of not doing this:

> *When an unclean spirit goes out of a man, he goes through dry places, seeking rest; and finding none, he says, "I will return to my house from which I came." And when he comes, he finds it swept and put in order. Then he goes and takes with him seven other spirits more wicked than himself, and they enter and dwell there; and the last state of that man is worse than the first.* (Luke 11:24–26)

When a demonic influence has been deposited into your life, not only must you remove it, but you also must realize that something will replace it. As a Christian, you need to be sure you replace it with a personal revelation of who God is in that area of your life. Information about God and His Word is not enough. I cannot urge you enough to get a copy of my book *Conquering Your Unseen Enemies*. It will thoroughly answer all questions you may have about the spiritual world of Satan and demons, and how WE WIN!

Above, we discussed how to replace demonic imagery. The same is true for every area of your life. For example, when you remove fear, replace it with the revelation of security in God's love, or you will revert back to fear. If the weight of worries and cares concern you, remove them from your life by committing them into the Lord's hands: *"Casting all your care upon Him, for He cares for you"* (1 Peter 5:7). Then be sure you replace the cares with the revelation of God's intimate concern for your well-being. You see, if you get rid of the cares but cannot see God caring for you, you will become an open vessel for the devil to dump more cares on you. Likewise, if you remove confusion and do not rely on the Lord as the Author of peace and wisdom, then you will go back to confusion again:

> *And let the peace of God rule in your hearts, to which also you were called in one body; and be thankful. Let the word of Christ dwell in you richly in all wisdom, teaching and admonishing one another in psalms and hymns and spiritual songs, singing with grace in your hearts to the Lord.* (Colossians 3:15–16)

But of Him you are in Christ Jesus, who became for us wisdom from God—and righteousness and sanctification and redemption.

(1 Corinthians 1:30)

If you do not substitute what Jesus died to give you in place of the demonic stronghold, you will only go back to it again. Fill yourself with the revelation of God and His Word. Diligently doing this throughout your life will prevent you from falling into these traps and needing to remove these demonic influences from your life. Nevertheless, if you find yourself falling prey to the devil, God will forgive you and give a new beginning to you, so you can live in freedom for the rest of your life! Hallelujah!

CHAPTER SEVEN

WHY FIGHT THE FEAR?

After reading the previous chapters, you may be asking, *Why is there so much to this thing called fear?* The answer is that the devil uses it as a major weapon to attack us. The enemy's target is God's purpose for our lives. In this chapter, we will discuss what fear has to do with your purpose.

Knowing God's purpose for your life is the key to this discussion. You see, the more you understand your spiritual purpose, the more you recognize the reason for your fears and challenges. If you examine your fears and challenges in light of your purpose, you will be able to identify their causes. This reveals why the devil is targeting you. His true reason for attacking you is to try to get you to abort your purpose!

Knowing this motivates you to defeat the devil. Otherwise, if you cannot see the cause of your conflicts, you can easily become discouraged, defeated, and dismayed. You must not succumb to that pressure, because its oppressive weight not only drives *you* down but also those around you, and it jeopardizes your purpose. The Bible encourages us with this promise: *"And let us not be weary in well doing: for in due season we shall reap, if we faint not"* (Galatians 6:9 KJV).

Recognizing your purpose and the cause of your conflicts, on the other hand, empowers you to rise above challenges with confidence to fulfill God's plan.

The Power of Purpose

Know to Whom and to What God Calls You

As Christians, we must recognize there is a purpose for our lives. We need to know to whom and to what God calls us. David understood this. Earlier we read the account in 1 Samuel 17 of David's confrontation with Goliath, the giant Philistine warrior. This story demonstrates the power of purpose. Now, let's reconsider it in light of this theme and examine the cause of his battle. I believe these new insights will help us to begin to face our challenges with new boldness and confidence!

Remember, the threats of one man, Goliath, were enough to cause the king and entire nation of Israel to fear: *"When Saul and all Israel heard those words of the Philistine* [Goliath], *they were dismayed, and greatly afraid"* (1 Samuel 17:11 KJV).

Although young David was still a shepherd at this time, the prophet Samuel had recently anointed him to become the next king of Israel. David's older brothers were already in the battle when David arrived to bring food at their father's request. Unlike the frightened Israelites, who acted upon what they heard from Goliath and ran at the sight of him, David took a different stand. He looked past the might of Goliath and acknowledged the mightier power of the living God. When David saw the war zone and heard Goliath's blasphemies, he recognized this was where God had called him to demonstrate His power. David sensed this was why God had anointed him, so he cried out, ready to do battle for the Lord.

> The enemy's power is small when compared with God's power.

However, the hiding Israelites agreed with each other that Goliath was too big for them to defeat. It was impossible. *David has no chance to succeed,* they thought. Even Eliab, David's oldest brother and soldier in Israel's army, overheard David's fearless reaction to Goliath and rebuked him. Eliab did not believe his youngest brother should be in the battle area, much less express confidence in his ability to defeat the Philistine monster! It is important for you not to surround yourself with people who continually question your

God-given ability to overcome that which appears humanly impossible. We will discuss more about this point in the next chapter.

Recognize the Cause of the Conflict in Relation to Your Purpose

Now, let's read how David responded to his brother's rebuke: *"And David said, 'What have I done now? Is there not a cause?'"* (1 Samuel 17:29). What was the cause? While Eliab and the nation of Israel saw the grounds for fear, David saw a cause. He saw the reason for this battle. It was to attack his purpose. In your life, you must understand why you stand up for moral principles, act differently from the crowd, or confront important issues. It is critical for you to recognize God's purpose, or you will not know what to do, much less have the tenacity to finish it. Instead, you will hide, paralyzed with fear. The devil uses fear to attack God's purpose for your life.

> You don't need a backup plan when you have God's plan.

If you do not know your purpose, it is likely that you will come up with other solutions or backup plans "in case God doesn't show up." That's rebellion, which is like *"the sin of witchcraft ["divination" NIV]"* (1 Samuel 15:23). It is the pagan activity of deciding what to do next based on anything other than God. Because Saul rebelled against God's plan in this way, he eventually lost his throne. Today, we have backup plans, too. For example, many people turn to bankruptcy to solve their financial problems or divorce court to end their marriage woes.

However, those who are fearless in God have no fallback positions, because they know they are running into battle for God's purpose. Since He has called them to fight, He will give the victory to them. Therefore, they have no reason to cower in fear or back down. David refused to be a part of Goliath's intimidation because he was willing to fight for God's kingdom. David recognized this was his purpose.

If you know your purpose and identify the cause of each challenge, you can defeat it, because you will see why it exists. I have learned a secret about life: The root determines the fruit. In other words, for everything apparent,

The root determines the fruit. something deeper is driving it. For everything we experience, something is causing it. Therefore, we must focus on the root of things, not their fruit. The fruit is merely the end product, but remember that fruit has seeds for the future. This principle also applies to demonic attacks. If you can see beyond the appearances of your challenges to what caused them, you can defeat them and confidently advance, thus fulfilling your purpose.

You must realize that the devil does not randomly select people with whom to pick fights. No, when he attacks, it is because he recognizes what God is doing. You see, no intelligent thief breaks into an empty warehouse. He enters only where he knows the valuables are. The devil is no different, because he is the biggest thief of all. For example, Jesus said in His parable of the sower,

The sower sows the word. And these are the ones by the wayside where the word is sown. When they hear, Satan comes immediately and takes away the word that was sown in their hearts. (Mark 4:14–15)

We are not ignorant of the devil's devices. We know his nature and why he acts against us. It is because Satan wants to abort God's purposes in His kingdom and our lives.

We have seen his insidious activity all throughout biblical history. For example, in the first chapter of Exodus, why did the king of Egypt want to kill all the baby boys of Israel when Moses was born? There was a cause. God's purpose for Moses was that he would deliverer Israel from their Egyptian bondage. Likewise, why did King Herod kill all the infant boys in Bethlehem about the age of baby Jesus? There was a cause. God had purposed Jesus to deliver the world from its spiritual bondage. You see, Satan is in the business of attempting to destroy God's deliverers and abort His plans. This includes you, and it included David.

Let's continue with David's story. Remember, at the time of this incident with Goliath, David had already been anointed to become the next king. Aware of God's plan for his life, David had a great desire to defend the people he would lead and be responsible for. If he could not stop Goliath at this point, how could he ever stop the enemy in the future to which God had called him?

Now, what cause did he see? What did David know that Israel did not? He recognized the reason Goliath was in that field. The devil was trying to defeat God, His people, and abort David's call to be their king.

That's why David considered Goliath a "reproach" or "disgrace" upon Israel and asked: *"Who is this uncircumcised Philistine that he should defy the armies of the living God?"* (1 Samuel 17:26 NIV).

Notice that David regarded Israel's armies not as those of King Saul. No, he considered them *"the armies of the living God"* Himself! When he called Goliath *"this uncircumcised Philistine,"* David meant the giant had no right to the land he and the other Philistines

> Satan seeks to destroy God's deliverers.

were living on. That was God's land for His covenant people. David recognized himself as God's champion in that hour. David would defend the people and territory for which God had anointed him. Knowing this, David boldly declared: *"Let no man's heart fail because of him; your servant will go and fight with this Philistine"* (verse 32).

In other words, David said, "Fear not. I am here. God has called and anointed me to fight this battle. This is part of my purpose."

What moved David on that battlefront was his purpose. Always remember, the highest motivation is purpose. The knowledge of your God-ordained purpose can cause you to soar above any obstacle. When you recognize that God has called you, you know He has equipped you and is with you. Nothing can stop you then!

God has called each of us to areas of responsibility and has delegated His authority to us to accomplish His plan. You have a territory, or realm of dominion, that God has given to you. One day in heaven, you will stand accountable to Him for it. Your responsibility depends on your areas of faithfulness and the particular call or anointing He has placed on your life. Your purpose is to walk in God's authority to accomplish His will for your life, whether it is in your home, community, local church, workplace, school, the government, the military, or other areas.

Remember, the enemy's activities against you have a cause. He is very intelligent. The more responsibility God gives to you, the greater the detriment

Satan will try to inflict to limit you. I encourage you today that as you move in your designated territories of responsibility and Satan attacks you, ask yourself, *Is there a cause for this fight?* If you are moving in God's plan for your life and God sends you into battle, go with confidence. Know that God has a purpose for you to fulfill and will give the victory to you!

Only Fight When God Calls You

As our ministry literally takes on new territories, we find ourselves fighting the devil on new fronts. For example, the men and women planting Bible schools faced great obstacles when our schools opened in Cambodia, Vietnam, and Burma. It was still illegal at that time to preach in areas of these nations. On every front, the devil engages us in new conflicts. Each time, I reexamine my heart, asking, *What did God say was my purpose? Is there a legitimate cause for me to fight this battle?* The answers to these questions determine whether I will fight. You see, I have learned that I should not fight unless legitimate causes exist. In other words, if God has not called and anointed me for certain battles, then I had better not go! They are not *my* battles to fight. The consequences of engaging in a battle that is not yours to fight can be severe.

We must know which battles to fight head-on. The following is a perfect example of knowing your God-ordained purpose and also knowing which battles are yours to fight and those that are not.

Several years ago, my son Eric and I, along with several other ministers, conducted a School of Ministry in Phnom Penh, Cambodia. A four-day open-air crusade for souls was to follow the training. We held the School of Ministry for the Christian workers and pastors in one of the smaller arenas at the massive Olympic Stadium in Phnom Penh. It was an awesome success. Literally hundreds accepted Jesus. We then trained them to evangelize and disciple the new converts, who would give their lives to Christ at the upcoming open-air crusade. My commitment was also to plant our School of Biblical Studies video Bible schools in Cambodia. At that time, *no* Bible schools like ours functioned in the entire nation.

Finally, it was time to preach to the masses at the crusade. That day, hundreds of thousands of lost people poured into the stadium from every direction to experience Jesus! The opening meeting was awesome.

I was thrilled to be scheduled to preach the crusade message the next night. However, at about midnight during my prayer time on that first night, I heard the Lord speak to me to leave Cambodia with the team early the next morning. To my shock, I heard Him say that the preacher and those on the platform would be killed if we did not obey and

> **Fight only the battles God wants you to fight.**

that there would not be another meeting in this crusade. I continued praying, rebuking the enemy, and asking God why.

Repeatedly, I heard Him answer that my purpose there was finished. We had planted the Bible schools and trained the people. However, I had a very difficult time believing that God was instructing us to leave. I am accustomed to persisting spiritually against all opposition and prevailing in Jesus' name.

Immediately, however, I gathered everyone on our team together and shared what I had heard from the Lord, asking each to pray earnestly. Unfortunately, our team was split. Part agreed with me that what I had heard was God, not fear, and that this spiritual battle was not ours to fight. In fact, God had already been speaking similarly to some of them. The others stated that no matter what happened, they would stay, pray, and prevail! Now, we had a great problem: a divided team, with both "sides" believing they were doing God's will!

Reluctantly, yet in obedience, those who heard what I had heard did leave early the next morning. Saying good-bye to the remainder of the team was very difficult. The question *Who had heard from God?* hung in the air as we departed with no natural reason to leave. Everything seemed perfect for us to continue the crusade. However, unknown to us, the Khmer Rouge, one of the most ruthless large-scale guerrilla terrorist groups in recent history, had vowed to kill the preacher—me! For the second meeting, they had laced the stadium with stolen military plastic explosive called C-4. The Khmer Rouge planned to kill as many as possible that night—not only me with all who were on the platform, but also the entire stadium of people who had come to the crusade! We had no earthly idea that tens of thousands of lives were in jeopardy.

Fortunately, another group, who knew of the Khmer Rouge's plans, swiftly intervened before the crusade began the next day. They took away in a personnel carrier all who were on the platform, driving them directly to the airport. These people had to stay there under military armed guard for their protection until the next morning when they were flown to safety in Thailand. The authorities immediately evacuated the stadium full of people and arrested some of the guerrilla terrorist group! Thank God, no lives were lost!

While all that happened, Eric and I were free! Hallelujah! It was Thanksgiving Day, so my son and I sat in a restaurant in Bangkok, Thailand, having a quiet turkey dinner. We could not call home from there because the telephones did not work. That's why we did not know what had happened until we landed in the United States, and I called Faye.

She immediately asked, "Gary, did you know you were on television?"

"No, what did I do?" I joked, not knowing any of this yet.

"You were preaching in that crusade," she explained, "and the guerrillas were going to kill everybody."

"Oh, yeah, that one," I replied easily. "Well, Eric and I are in Dallas, Texas, and all the people who left with us are safe. We're all fine." It was now clear that I had, in fact, heard from God about leaving Cambodia, and there were no more meetings in that crusade. Truly, this was not my battle to fight.

Eventually, several years later, Pol Pot, the brutal leader of the Khmer Rouge, died and the group disbanded and surrendered. During its reign in Cambodia, the Khmer Rouge was responsible for the deaths of approximately two million people.[20]

Do you see why it is vital to know which battles are yours? Your purpose and even your very life could be in jeopardy. This is true not only today but also since man's creation. For example, consider Abraham. He fought some fights that were not his. You may recall that God had promised to make him a great nation (which would become Israel) and had called him to leave his country:

Now the LORD *had said to Abram [Abraham]: "Get out of your country, from your family and from your father's house, to a land that I will show*

20. "Khmer Rouge" and "Pol Pot." The Britannica Concise (Merriam-Webster and Encyclopedia Britannica, 2000; Yahoo!, 2002). <http://education.yahoo.com/search/be?lb=t&p=url%3Ak/khmer _rouge> and <http://education.yahoo.com/search/be?lb=t&p=url%3Ap/pol_pot> (28 May 2002).

you. I will make you a great nation; I will bless you and make your name
great; and you shall be a blessing." (Genesis 12:1–2)

That was Abraham's purpose: to become the father of Israel. Now, what
did he do? "*So Abram departed as the* LORD *had spoken to him, and Lot went*
with him. And Abram was seventy-five years old when he departed from Haran"
(verse 4).

Abraham obeyed God but only in part. Notice that he took his nephew
Lot with him even though God had distinctly told Abraham to leave his kin-
dred. That meant he was to leave his nephew at home.

Consequently, Lot caused Abraham "a lot" of
challenges! You see, after he left his country, most
of the battles Abraham fought related to Lot and
not God's plan for Abraham. They were not his
but Lot's to fight. For example, on one occasion,
King Chedorlaomer of Elam and several other
kings captured Lot as they conquered Sodom and

> Choosing to
> obey just a little
> can lead to a lot
> of trouble.

Gomorrah.[21] When Abraham heard this news, he launched into the conflict and
recovered his nephew, the goods, and the people. Abraham would not have been
involved in that fight if Lot had stayed at home! Lot also created for Abraham
numerous other battles, which distracted his uncle from his God-given purpose.

Let me ask you: Are you fighting some unnecessary battles? Think about
it. If God has not given a certain responsibility to you, then you do not have
the authority to fight for that area. It is not your battle. If you enter it, the
cause of that conflict will not be well-defined. Consequently, it will distract
you and put at risk the fulfillment of your purpose and maybe even your life.
I urge you to examine your conflicts for legitimate causes to be sure you have
not disobediently carried "a Lot" with you!

Go with God

Now, this was not David's circumstance. God had chosen him for such a time
as this. David had a purpose. He was to lead this army of the living God into

---

21. See Genesis 14.

victory. There was no reason to fear, because David also recognized Goliath's cause. The evil giant did not defy David, Saul, or the Israelite army. Instead, he actually defied the living God and His covenant with His chosen people. The giant had to contend, not with David, but with the God whom David served. Those who engage God's children in conflict ultimately defy God and must battle Him.

> You can defeat your giant when you rely on God.

David knew that God was more than able to defend Himself. He would be with David as he walked in his divine purpose to defeat God's enemies. Therefore, David did not need any carnal help in this battle. Remember, Saul offered his armor to David to fight Goliath. However, David refused it, taking only a slingshot and five smooth stones, knowing God was with him. David went on to defeat Goliath by cutting off the warrior's head with his own sword. When the Israelite army saw the dead giant, they rallied and went on to defeat the fleeing Philistine garrison.

David knew something Saul and their fellow countrymen did not: his God-given purpose. When you know your divine purpose, you, too, can defeat any giant that arises to challenge you and your God!

Confidence in Purpose

All throughout history, God's anointed ones, who knew their divine purposes, defeated their enemies against great odds. Another example is the prophet Elisha. He had the capacity and resilience to obey God in the face of adversity because he, like David, knew his purpose.

Elisha's Supernatural Vision

Second Kings 6 tells one of the many instances in which Elisha walked in his purpose as God's prophet. This story not only clearly depicts the power of purpose, but it also demonstrates how fear results from relying on the arm of flesh, believing information as it naturally appears, and trusting in the sensory reaction of human sight.

During this period, Israel was at war with Syria. Repeatedly, God supernaturally revealed to Elisha the Syrians' battle plans, which the man of God then reported to his Israelite king. Realizing their strategies were somehow being divulged to Israel, the king of Syria demanded that his men find the traitor who was spying on them. The soldiers informed their king that the man responsible for the leakage of Syrian strategic secrets was not a spy in their camp, but the Israelite prophet Elisha. The king then furiously plotted Elisha's capture and death. He sent a great army to seek and kill this one man! Arriving at night, the soldiers sneaked in to surround the city of Dothan, where Elisha and his servant were.

Early the next morning, when Elisha's servant discovered the Syrian army encircling them, his initial reaction was one of anxiety and fear:

And when the servant of the man of God arose early and went out, there was an army, surrounding the city with horses and chariots. And his servant said to him, "Alas, my master! What shall we do?" (2 Kings 6:15)

In other words, the servant frantically asked, "What are we going to do? Look, the Syrian army is against us. There are two of us, and look what they have!" Suddenly, they were at war: just Elisha and his servant against the Syrian army. From the servant's weak, human perspective, the odds seemed insurmountable because he was relying on the arm of flesh.

Think about it: Elisha had an army launched against him. He must have had the devil's attention! Why? The devil could see Elisha's purpose. The prophet of God was a serious threat and, therefore, worthy of an army's assault in the enemy's eyes. The cause of this conflict was to prevent Elisha from fulfilling his God-given purpose. Here we see the devil again trying to defeat God, His people, and abort the call of the man of God.

Now, Elisha knew his purpose and the cause of the conflict, so he was not concerned that enemy horses and chariots had trapped them on the mountain. If he had believed information as it naturally appeared, Elisha could have worried, screaming, "Oh, no, we're going to die!" However, he did not. Elisha knew their apparent situation was not real but False Evidence Appearing Real. Elisha calmly responded, *"Do not fear, for those who are with us are more than those who are with them"* (2 Kings 6:16).

Elisha did not rely on his sensory reaction of sight. He did not see merely the horses, chariots, and all the army. He saw something more and wanted his servant to see it, too. So Elisha prayed,

"LORD, I pray, open his eyes that he may see." Then the LORD opened the eyes of the young man, and he saw. And behold, the mountain was full of horses and chariots of fire all around Elisha. (2 Kings 6:17)

Hidden from human eyes, God's angelic army, horses, and chariots of fire, surrounded Elisha on the mountain. While the servant saw what *appeared* to be, Elisha looked at how it *really* was. The prophet saw the Syrian army, not as a mighty force, but merely as a group of puny men wielding swords, spears, and shields, with horses and chariots. They could not match the strength of almighty God's heavenly army!

Your Confidence in God

When you walk in your purpose, you can have confidence in God. This enables you to see beyond the natural realm to recognize there are more with you than against you. Yes, through negative appearances, the enemy will attempt to demoralize you, but when you walk in the power of your purpose, God's Spirit will empower you with the confidence to conquer your trials.

> Walk in the Power of your purpose.

Do not think your conflicts are against you personally. No, the battles you face are not really yours but the Lord's. The enemy attacks God's objectives, and you happen to be in the middle of it all! This is the reason you can face any challenge with confidence. Fear not, because the One you know is highly capable of defeating His enemies. He and His angelic forces are with you in battle. That's all you need. When you grasp this revelation, faith and confidence will erupt in your spirit. You will be able to declare, "I know God's purpose for my life, and I recognize the cause of this conflict." Then you can make fear bow and confidently defeat the enemy's attacks regardless of the natural odds against you.

Walk Confidently in Your Purpose

Always remember that before the foundation of the earth, God had you in His mind. He ordained and destined you for a purpose. The Bible declares:

Who hath saved us, and called us with an holy calling, not according to our works, but according to his own purpose and grace, which was given us in Christ Jesus before the world began. (2 Timothy 1:9 KJV)

God has dispatched legions of angels to support you in everything you are to accomplish for Him. He has given His Word and power to lead and defend you. Do you realize that the enemy is terrified of you because of this awesome backing you have? The devil knows that if you fulfill your purpose by walking in obedience to God, he and his demons will no longer be able to operate within your environment. You have that much power and authority at your disposal! Therefore, it is time to walk confidently in God's purpose for your life, despite the enemy's assaults. It is time to be an active Christian and obey God. You cannot afford to be idle or to cower in fear.

God Desires Exploits

Today, I encourage you to examine your life. Be honest with yourself. Does it consist of fear, negativity, and worry instead of exploits for God? Do you seem to find reasons why you cannot go to the battlefront and win, or why things do not work for you? If so, you need to get in tune with God's purpose for your life and walk in it with confidence.

Our Father needs His children to do exploits in this generation. These works will require a very special and unique caliber of individual because conventional ways of working for God will no longer be effective in these end days. Methods of communication will be different. We will have to take new risks in areas of conflict. God will try us to determine our motivations, attitudes, and perspectives. He will examine us to see if we speak life or fear.

In these times, God and the body of Christ need you to know the cause for which you are fighting. We need you to have the conviction in your heart that says, "I am willing to do whatever it takes to obey God's purpose for my life."

In the School of Biblical Studies, we have a course called *Power Principles of Prayer*. In it, we instruct the students to pray Ephesians 1:16–23 ten times

> Know the cause for which you are fighting.

every day for the Holy Spirit to reveal in their hearts the person of Jesus and His purpose. The apostle Paul prayed this for the New Testament church. Likewise, we need to pray it for ourselves today. Once you receive this revelation, it will change the course of your life and help you to know your purpose! Pray it now:

> *I…cease not to give thanks for you, making mention of you in my prayers; that the God of our Lord Jesus Christ, the Father of glory, may give unto you the spirit of wisdom and revelation in the knowledge of him: the eyes of your understanding being enlightened; that ye may know what is the hope of his calling, and what the riches of the glory of his inheritance in the saints, and what is the exceeding greatness of his power to us-ward who believe, according to the working of his mighty power, which he wrought in Christ, when he raised him from the dead, and set him at his own right hand in the heavenly places, far above all principality, and power, and might, and dominion, and every name that is named, not only in this world, but also in that which is to come: and hath put all things under his feet, and gave him to be the head over all things to the church, which is his body, the fulness of him that filleth all in all.* (Ephesians 1:15–23 KJV)

CHAPTER EIGHT

KNOW THE FEAR FACTOR OF YOUR FAMILY AND FRIENDS

Are you walking with valiant or fearful people? This question is critical because fearful people can sway you into fear even after you have become free. To stay free of fear, you must recognize the fear factor of your family, friends, and affiliations.

Do you associate with people who are valiant in spirit and have a conquering consciousness or with those who are limited and restrained? Are the people around you continually cautious, wary, and concerned? Do their challenges paralyze them with worry? Or do you associate with people who know the Lord's voice when they hear it, "throw caution to the winds," and engage their faith to do His exploits? Do they persistently appropriate the Word of God correctly and experience the kind of breakthroughs we read about in His Word? Do they move in God's limitless ability to the extent that even the world recognizes His power in their lives?

In this chapter, we will examine people's relationships with those who are fearful and those who are valiant. We will see that some people move in fear, while others launch out in the dauntless spirit of faith. The differences between the two types will be clear. This will help you to see the effects that your associations have on you. I believe the Holy Spirit will expose the error of some of your relationships. You may see in a new light your personal inter-actions at home, work, and church, as well as gain insight about the way you communicate with others.

God is looking for bold, fearless people who have a tenacity to run with His vision despite the odds. He is looking for people to step beyond the aver-age to do exploits in the name of Jesus. These acts of faith will not necessar-ily occur on public platforms or on crusade grounds.

> Acting in faith puts you on God's side.

They can happen in your home, workplace, school, and neighborhood. God is looking for *you!*

He might call you to break some bad relationships with friends or workers who expect you to compro-mise. But always remember: *"If God is for us, who can be against us?"* (Romans 8:31).

Maybe you need to take a moral stand, saying, "No! I know in my heart that's sin, and I will not have any part of it." Words like these may cause the people you affiliate with to criticize or even ostracize you. However, taking a stand will move you over the threshold of fear and put you on God's side. It will place you in the valiant zone of faith.

False Safety versus Valiant Faith

When faced with difficult circumstances, some people choose to hide in what they believe is a place of safety when, in reality, it is a zone of fear. Although it may appear to be their comfort zone, it is the worst place to be because it is outside God's protection. Living in the valiant zone of faith is the key to true safety and overcoming life's challenges. To help you determine if you live in the false safety zone of fear or the valiant zone of faith, let's examine several biblical examples.

Saul and the Israelites Hid in the Back Bush

The book of 1 Samuel tells the story of an Israelite-Philistine conflict in which the Israelites faced discouraging odds. At that time, Philistine garri-sons enslaved the Israelites throughout the nation. Let's read how this hea-then army readied for battle:

Then the Philistines gathered together to fight with Israel, thirty thousand chariots and six thousand horsemen, and people as the sand which is on the seashore in multitude. And they came up and encamped in Michmash, to the east of Beth Aven. (1 Samuel 13:5)

Picture the magnitude of the conflict here. The Israelites, under King Saul, faced great odds. Their army numbered only three thousand. Before them stood their enemy, the Philistines, with thirty thousand chariots, six thousand horsemen, and a multitude of people. Outnumbered in every way, the Israelites needed a giant breakthrough.

How did they react? Did the Israelites retreat to the false safety zone of fear or advance into the valiant zone of faith? The next verse quickly answers this question.

When the men of Israel saw that they were in a strait, (for the people were distressed,) then the people did hide themselves in caves, and in thickets, and in rocks, and in high places, and in pits. And some of the Hebrews went over Jordan to the land of Gad and Gilead. As for Saul, he was yet in Gilgal, and all the people followed him trembling. (verses 6–7 KJV)

What did the Israelites see? They looked at all their enemy's chariots, horsemen, and soldiers who could not be numbered. They focused on the magnitude of their conflict and became distraught, anxious, worried, discouraged, and fearful. Likewise, many of us look at our opposition and begin to count our enemies. For example, three failed job interviews, two divorces, six enemies, two auto accidents, and so forth unsettle us. We see too many chariots, horsemen, and foot soldiers, and we feel hemmed in on all sides.

Now, how did the people follow King Saul? They trembled in fear. The immediate reaction of the much smaller Israelite army was to hide, seeking shelter in their imaginary false comfort zone of fear. For them, their safety zone became caves, thickets, rocks, high places, and pits. Taking solace in fear, they likely found satisfaction in the knowledge that many others also locked themselves in this arena.

> Hiding provides no real solace.

Notice here that the Philistines had not yet attacked the Israelites. In fact, Jonathan, King Saul's son, had just valiantly led a portion of the Israelite army in a successful raid on a Philistine garrison.[22] The Israelites not only hid *before* their enemies attacked but also *after* they had just won a battle against the Philistines!

You see, despite the circumstances, the fearful find comfort in hiding. When people live in the false safety zone of fear, they often retreat before their enemies attack. They begin mapping out alternatives based on their anticipation of the worst, asking, "What if God does not show up?" They take cover behind anything. Usually they find room to hide under other people's excuses and lifestyles. They cower under their own inability, justifying themselves because of their inadequacies. Today they hide behind excuses ranging from raising children to money matters. They do whatever it takes to stay out of the fray.

As with the Israelites, when people today face insurmountable odds and hide in the false security of fear, often they build around themselves associations of people who also use fear as a defense mechanism. They carry on conversations and establish relationships that cause them to feel secure in what they are afraid of. Fear causes them to cluster with people at work, in their families, in the local church, and elsewhere to create atmospheres of security. These places feel safe to them because they give no one access who will expose the secret hold fear has on their hearts or encourage them to break through its barriers. There is false comfort in associating with the fearful.

Do you know people who, when facing confrontation, retreat in fear? Do you know those who have promises from God but are hiding from moving in those promises? If so, they adamantly give reasons why they should hide in their caves, thickets, rocks, high places, and pits. We all face thresholds of fear, and if we fail to cross them, we will find opportunities to hide. However, the zone of fear brings with it a false sense of security because we are the most vulnerable there.

Do You Live in the Battlefront of Glory?

Despite God's promises, are *you* hiding from what He wants *you* to do? Are you finding a false safe haven in fear, naming what you think are valid

---

22. See 1 Samuel 13:3–4.

reasons to justify your retreat from His directives? Are you using excuses to escape God's will and creating backup plans in spite of His assurance that He will see you through? You must realize that you cannot live in the false comfort zone of fear with others and see God fulfill His will in your life. You cannot take the path of least resistance, walking in fear, and expect to accomplish great feats for God. Risks and discomfort come with working in His kingdom! Other-wise, you would not have to walk in faith.

Often, I take mission teams into developing countries, such as Guatemala, for a month at a time. We take risks and live in uncomfortable environments. For example, have you ever slept on a dirt floor for three or four days? Have you had rats, the size of your foot, running all over you, so much that you begin to think they know your middle name? Have you had them examine you in the middle of the night, sniffing your ear, while you wondered if they were hungry? I have experienced this.

Your answer might be, "Oh, no, I'll *never* get in *that* environment!"

Why not? Is it because you live in your caves, thickets, rocks, high places, and pits? Do you live in your carefully selected false security zones? Do only *you* decide where you will live and go? You ought to live only where God would have you to live. Let me ask you an important question: Do you live in the battlefront of glory or the back bush of hiding? Are you fighting the fight of faith and bringing glory to God on the battlefront, or are you cowering in the back bush, hiding from the fray God has called you into?

> Are you living by faith or hiding in fear?

Israel's Disadvantage

Now, let's return to the account of the Israelite-Philistine battle. Remember, the Israelites, under King Saul, hid in fear. Besides the huge numerical advantage that the Philistine army enjoyed, they also denied the Israelites access to effective weaponry: *"Now there was no blacksmith to be found throughout all the land of Israel, for the Philistines said, 'Lest the Hebrews make swords or spears'"* (1 Samuel 13:19). Remember at this time the Philistines enslaved the Israelites and therefore controlled their access to blacksmiths, a strategic source of weapons. However, the Israelites did what they could. *"But all the Israelites would go down to the Philistines to sharpen each man's plowshare, his mattock, his ax, and his sickle"* (verse 20). Since the Israelites could not have weapons, they sharpened their farm tools! That's all they had to fight with.

> *So it came about, on the day of battle, that there was neither sword nor spear found in the hand of any of the people who were with Saul and Jonathan. But they were found with Saul and Jonathan his son. And the garrison of the Philistines went out to the pass of Michmash.*
>
> (verses 22–23)

Only King Saul and his son, Jonathan, possessed any weapons of war. Think about it. Only two soldiers, each with a sword or spear, in the entire nation of Israel faced the Philistines' thirty thousand chariots, six thousand horsemen, and so many armed men they could not number them!

To the natural mind, it makes sense to hide. That is why the sword in Saul's hand was useless. Relying on his natural instinct to hide in fear, he refused to fight or lead the Israelites into battle. Jonathan had already proven himself valiant in battle. Now, he held the only available sword in all of Israel. In this environment, it entered into Jonathan's heart to fight the Philistines!

Jonathan's Battlefront of Glory

The next chapter in 1 Samuel portrays a key moment when valor and faith produced glory for God and victory for His people. God tested Jonathan's faith as he faced the enormous, overwhelming Philistine army. The chapter opens with Jonathan explaining his battle plan to the young man who carried his armor for him:

> *Now it happened one day that Jonathan the son of Saul said to the young man who bore his armor, "Come, let us go over to the Philistines' garrison that is on the other side." But he did not tell his father.* (1 Samuel 14:1)

Notice that when Jonathan was ready to make his stand, he did not tell his doubting father, because he knew Saul was sense-dominated, as was their army. Under Saul's fearful leadership, Israel's army had dwindled to only 600 men at this point. Jonathan knew that associating with fearful people would draw him back, so he chose the only person who would go into battle with him. That was *not his father!*

Do Not Tell the "Thicket Hiders"

To win your battles, you must know with whom to align or disconnect yourself. When you are planning to carry out exploits of fearless faith, do not ask for help from the people hiding in the thickets. What can they do for you? You must not take the "Sauls" of this world with you into battle. If you do, their presence alone can cause you to lose your fight. Not only was Saul fearful, but also remember that God had removed His hand from the king because of his rebellion.[23] No matter who they are, you cannot afford to take fearful, rebellious people with you when you enter the Lord's work!

In fact, you should not even consult them. When you are advancing, do not inform people who are retreating. What can they offer you? Do not discuss the Holy Spirit's plans with the fearful because they will try to drag you back into fear. If they are negative, even your family, friends, and fellow church members might try to talk you out of obeying God, especially if what He wants you to do appears to them to be risky. Their negativity and fear can affect you.

Have you ever watched negative people? Wherever they go, they bring their clouds of fear with them. You can become negative and fearful along with them simply through your conversations with them. Think about it. What happens when you talk with someone who is depressed? If you don't lift him up, he will drag you down!

Fearful people might warn you, "I wouldn't try that."

Answer them, "Well, why not? I won't be doing it; the Lord will." Then quote this verse to them: *"I can do all things through Christ who strengthens me"* (Philippians 4:13).

They might say, "Oh, brother, I'd be careful."

"Not me," tell them. "The Bible says to be carefree. Yes! *'Be careful for nothing; but in every thing by prayer and supplication with thanksgiving let your requests be made known unto God'"* (verse 6 KJV).

---

23. See 1 Samuel 15.

"Well, you'd better take it easy."

Answer them, "No, I will '*take it by force*'" (Matthew 11:12).

"You'd better slow down," the fearful might say.

"Oh, why should I do that? Jesus said to work while it is yet day because '*the night is coming when no one can work*'" (John 9:4).

"Well, you just can't expect God to do everything."

"Why not? He's done a good job so far. He just needs people who can trust Him with their whole hearts. The Bible says, '*Trust in the* LORD *with all your heart, and lean not on your own understanding; in all your ways acknowledge Him, and He shall direct your paths*' (Proverbs 3:5–6). That's what I am doing!"

Answers like this should shut down any pessimistic and fearful conversations! You must recognize fear and negativity when you encounter it. Then deal with it as an enemy. Shut down its access to you.

Maybe the Lord Will Work for Us by a Few

Next, let's continue to read about Jonathan's battle against the Philistines:

Then Jonathan said to the young man who bore his armor, "Come, let us go over to the garrison of these uncircumcised; it may be that the LORD *will work for us. For nothing restrains the* LORD *from saving by many or by few."* (1 Samuel 14:6)

> You and God equals victory.

At that time, it was down to two men, Jonathan and his armorbearer, with one weapon, against an enemy garrison. Yet Jonathan was sure the two of them would prevail with God on their side. It is always important to know who is with you.

However, notice that Jonathan said, "*It may be that the* LORD *will work for us*" (emphasis added). Basically, he said to his armorbearer, "Let's go to the other side. If the Lord is with us, we will prevail. If not, this garrison of Philistines will kill us. Are you ready to go?" Jonathan was determined to move out with conviction without knowing the outcome. In Jonathan's heart, he believed that God was in the business of victory, and the two of them could win with God on their side.

Now, look again at the last phrase in verse 6. Here Jonathan's statement was critical. He said, "*Nothing restrains the* LORD *from saving by many or by few*" (emphasis added). He realized that if God was present, it did not require masses in agreement for God to deliver them and perform His Word. Jonathan simply moved into battle with unconditional faith, knowing that victory or defeat rested upon the extent to which God was with his armorbearer and him. The issue for Jonathan was not the number of soldiers with him, but who they were and who God is.

Know the Nature of God and the People with You

What was the armorbearer's answer to this great challenge? He agreed to be with Jonathan according to what was in Jonathan's heart. He said, "*Do all that is in your heart. Go then; here I am with you, according to your heart*" (1 Samuel 14:7).

As Jonathan built a relationship with his armorbearer, their hearts connected. Instead of telling this risky battle plan to his father, the king of Israel, Jonathan told his armorbearer! This speaks volumes. Whom he associated with was also an indication of his level of faith in God! Jonathan knew the nature of God *and* the nature of his armorbearer.

> Associate with people of great faith.

You must know the nature of the people with you! Associate with people according to their faith or fear of heart. When working for God, you do not need many important and powerful people to help you. God can do the work through you with many as well as He can with a few. Look for people, no matter who they are or how few they are, who are with you in God's plans according to your heart. Look for those who anchor themselves in faith, not fear.

You see, most people wait to determine how well it works before they decide if they will do the Lord's work with you. They think, *The Lord go with you, and if He shows up, I might follow. If not, may God bless you as you die.* If you were facing a demonic attack today, do you know some people you could call who would agree with you in faith against the unbelief, doubt, and fear. Would they support you as you stood up to the challenge? Unfortunately, you probably know many people who would attempt to talk you out of fighting the fight of faith.

Now, think for a moment. If I asked you to name the people who would be willing to risk all to be with you in following God according to your heart, how many names would be on that list? You probably can count them on one hand, and maybe only on one finger! If you have ever faced a critical conflict in your Christian walk, this is why only you and maybe one or two other people agreed that God would move on your behalf. Such people are with you according to your heart.

These are the two types of people with whom we can become involved. Not many are willing to rise above fear to walk in faith against all odds. God is looking for people who are valiant, tenacious, and fearless to do His exploits. If you want to answer God's call, then surround yourself with others who will do the same, even if it is only one person! Do not let the fearful have access to your heart.

My wife, Faye, and I experienced this when we went through our divorce from each other. I knew that God was going to reconcile our marriage, and I was confident that we would remarry each other. I warned her not to fellowship with certain women who also were going through divorces. Faye maintained that these women were Spirit-filled, solid Christians, one of whom had led her to Christ. However, they constantly communicated their fears and misery, rehearsing how poorly their husbands had treated them. Like many groups of people, these women were fleeing with the fleeing. Their dismal response to marriage suggested a retreat that was simply not my retreat. Throughout this time, I learned how to pray effectively. As a result, Faye did not want to be in that group of women again. Hallelujah! She found that, in order to have our marriage restored, she had to break off her involvement with them. Soon afterward, Faye and I remarried each other.

You must decide with whom you will associate. Choose people who surrender their lives to God's authority and affiliate themselves with people of faith, not fear.

The Lord Worked a Victory

We read that Jonathan decided to fight the Philistines, and his armor-bearer agreed to go with him according to his heart. Now, when the two of them went, God worked a supernatural victory. He caused the Philistines to fall into great fear; there was *"trembling in the camp"* (1 Samuel 14:15). The entire garrison fled the battlefield! What happened next is no surprise:

> *Likewise all the men of Israel who had hidden in the mountains of Ephraim, when they heard that the Philistines fled, they also followed hard after them in the battle. So the LORD saved Israel that day, and the battle shifted to Beth Aven.*   (1 Samuel 14:22–23)

Remember, earlier we discussed that most people wait to see how well you do before they join in the Lord's work. That happened here. Because it went well for Jonathan and his armorbearer, the fearful Israelites suddenly became bold enough to help! However, if the two had not been successful, they would have died without any help from their countrymen. That is why you should not take the fearful with you into battle.

> Don't go into battle with fearful companions.

All you need is God! However, if you do bring others with you, take only those who have the conviction to run with His vision despite the risks.

God led Jonathan in victory over the Philistines that day. He and his armorbearer did an exploit. They defeated an entire garrison of Philistines. Despite the impossible odds, something inside Jonathan's heart caused him to prevail over fear. That something was his faith in God's power. This was Jonathan's battlefront of glory.

Jonathan's armorbearer shared his master's faith and followed after Jonathan's valiant heart. Consider carefully those with whom *you* associate. Are they fearful or valiant? Do they share your faith? Will they reinforce your valor or induce fear into your life?

Jonathan's armorbearer understood an important principle about going into battle. He knew he had to be in agreement with Jonathan's heart if he planned to go into battle with him. This was a life-or-death decision, and he had to be committed to participate in Jonathan's valor. Not many people are willing to make this commitment.

That is why you don't see great numbers of people eagerly pursuing life's risks on the mission field. Many people enjoy their comfortable lives too much.

They wonder why they should risk their lives for people who will not benefit them. What glory is there in such trips? What reward is there? Why risk the dangers? Such questions are typical and reflect the type of life many people live.

Souls Knit Together

Have you noticed that people who are valiant in God have a different edge to them? You cannot have long cave-, thicket-, and pit-hiding conversations with them! I cannot picture Jonathan agreeing with others that winning was impossible. We read earlier about David, who slew the giant Goliath. I like his attitude and spirit of valiance. Jonathan and David were similar. Would they provoke *you* to good works, if you were in Saul's army, or would they intimidate you?

Jonathan's and David's valiant spirits made them unique in Israel but very similar to each other. A shared faith and valor creates a dynamic bond among people. Because of this, Jonathan's and David's souls became closely knit. After David cut off Goliath's head and the Israelites won the battle with the Philistines, Jonathan and David met with Saul. The Bible says, *"Now when he had finished speaking to Saul, the soul of Jonathan was knit to the soul of David, and Jonathan loved him as his own soul"* (1 Samuel 18:1).

I like this. The Spirit of God connected Jonathan to David in profound love. Think about it. What did Jonathan and David have in common? One, they did not keep company with fearful Saul and his men. Two, they boldly engaged in battle despite insurmountable odds, trusting only in God.

> **Shared faith and valor bond people to each other.**

Therefore, when Jonathan saw in David the same spirit of God's victory that he had, their souls knitted together. They became great friends, their hearts in one accord with God's conquering Spirit.

Rooted in their fearless spirits, the love between Jonathan and David even touched Saul.

Saul took him [David] that day, and would not let him go home to his father's [Jesse's] house anymore. Then Jonathan and David made a covenant, because he loved him as his own soul. And Jonathan took off the robe that was on him and gave it to David, with his armor, even to his sword and his bow and his belt. (1 Samuel 18:2–4)

Here Jonathan was not simply loaning David his clothes and weapons. No, when Jonathan stripped himself of his robe, he literally was turning over his birthright to David. This is important because Jonathan's birthright, as Saul's oldest son, was the throne of Israel. Jonathan was next in line to be the king of Israel, yet he took off all his personal royalty and clothed David with it. With this gesture, Jonathan was giving up his future kingship to David! Eventually, David became king after Jonathan and Saul died. Those who were in Saul's regime then came under David.

You see, if you live in agreement with God, you will recognize others in similar agreement. Your spirit knows godly strength, confidence, and conviction when it sees these characteristics in others. That's why you yearn to be with these kinds of people.

A Tested Life Is a Trusted Life

When an incident breaks you through all resistance, catapulting you over the threshold of fear, you no longer care about losing your false safety zone. Your thicket and pit life is not important anymore. Your backup plan and second choice (in case God does not show up) are meaningless because you have turned to God as your only Source. You have trusted Him and passed His test. Now, God's trust in you is evident, and so others also will trust you!

That is what happened when Jonathan and David rejected the human urge to hide in the bushes. By refusing to conform to human limitations, they drew upon God's infinite power. They broke through thresholds of fear, rejecting the need for others' recognition and the temptation to measure their odds according to human standards. With only faith in God, they ran into battle, making Him their Source. Through their individual tests, Jonathan and David proved they trusted God unconditionally.

On the other hand, the cynical Saul failed his test. Jonathan and David recognized they could not trust Saul with God's plans. Therefore, Jonathan did not ask him for help, and David rejected his armor, running into battle only with the armor of God. It is impossible to know what the fearful will do in difficult circumstances. They might stand, run, turn, or even shoot you. It is better not to include them at all in your plans for God's work.

However, you *can* trust those who pass God's tests. You can join them in doing exploits for the kingdom of God. In fact, you need to *look* for these people who repeatedly cross the thresholds of their greatest fears. Seek those who display valor and wisdom in battle. Watch for people who do not appear distracted or disillusioned regardless of pressure. Search for those who see God's causes as worthy of fighting and even dying for. These people will usually be in the thick of a battle even though they may be in the realm of uncertainty. However, God always shows up for them, while many unconnected onlookers wonder, *How did God do that?* Build relationships with those who forsake every human endeavor for the kingdom of God, refusing to compromise His Word. Align yourself with those who have demonstrated valiant faith and trust that God will do what He promises. These people have passed God's tests. Always remember, a tested life is a trusted life.

Commit to Strengthen Each Other

> Associating with valiant people infuses you with courage.

When your spirit identifies and connects with the valiant in faith, you become bolder and more authoritative for God. Your heart engages with fellow Christians to do exploits for God's kingdom. Personally, my heart connects for God's purposes with my wife, my children, those in my church, and many people around the world whom I lead and minister beside. We engage in God's work together, strongly connecting with each other in Christ. Nothing can undo our commitment to each other except death. I often state to my family and those with whom I engage in God's work, "I will never leave you. The only way our relationship can end is if you leave me." This statement should be the philosophy of all Christians' lives. Find those who will help you to stay strong in faith and valor. An excellent example of this is one of our mission trips to Kenya.

My Battlefront of Glory in Kenya

When we went to Kenya several years ago for a crusade, the Anti-Christ Cult there threatened us. The group vowed to kill me to prove that Christ did not resurrect from the dead. If He did resurrect, they maintained, then so would I after they shot me! This was an open-air crusade in a huge field with no fences or tickets. Anyone could come, including the cult members.

As we were in the country preparing for the crusade, a Kenyan military guard began to beat on the door of my hotel room. When I answered, I saw his machine gun, big metal helmet, metal jacket, armor on his shoes, and shield! He looked like he was ready for war.

"Are you Reverend Whetstone?" he asked.

"Yes."

"The cult is going to kill you," he succinctly informed me.

"When?"

"At 6:00 P.M." Then he explained what the cult had just done. "They smashed up the car your man drove to check on the crusade field. They broke the windshield and smashed the doors, front and back ends, and fenders. They kicked in the car, threw stones, and beat it with sticks."

"Is my man all right?"

"Yeah, he got out," the guard answered.

"Fine, then we will go have a crusade!" I quickly replied.

"No! No! You don't understand. These people are going to shoot you at 6:00!" he insisted. "We ask you for the cause of peace in Nairobi, Kenya, don't go! We can't protect you. There are only four of us dressed like this."

"Okay," I answered, "let me pray to see what God says."

When I asked the Lord what He wanted me to do, He clearly told me, "I did not tell you to come here to quit. I told you to come here to preach." That's all I needed to know! Instead of giving in to the cult or to the guard's warnings, I decided to hold the crusade.

I called my team together and alerted them of the possibility that the cult would shoot us at the crusade. "There are a thousand cult members scheduled to be armed," I explained, "and we are the targets. I want you to hear from God individually about whether to go with me. If you want to go to the crusade, you will stand on the platform with me. If you don't want to go, then stay in your hotel room to pray."

> Being around
> fearful people
> can increase
> your fear.

Those were the two choices I gave because I knew that many of the team were scared and hesitant. I did not want them to walk onto the platform with the fear of death. If they visualized death in that situation, they would begin to believe they would die and would act accordingly. I personally could not afford for them to do this because I knew that associating with fearful people could intensify the degree of fear in my life and make me concerned for them. On the other hand, I would enhance my ability to overcome fear by having only those who were valiant around me.

In anticipation of potential challenges, I had instructed my mission team earlier that it was important for them to pray to hear from God about how and when they would die. Otherwise, they would needlessly perceive their deaths in numerous other false situations. The Bible says: *"And as it is appointed for men to die once, but after this the judgment"* (Hebrews 9:27). Each of us must know when his appointment is because the fear of death is a great snare to man.[24]

That day in Kenya, I assured my team, "I know I will not die tonight." The Lord had shown my death to me, and I knew it was not then. "Now," I continued, "that does not eliminate the possibility of being shot, but it *does* mean I won't die from any wounds here."

Privately, I considered the options. God instructed me to preach, so leaving was not a choice. I knew I would not die then. However, I might get shot. What would that be like? Considering the cult, I thought, *Well, they probably aren't very accurate shots. So if they fired, they would likely hit me in the shoulder, not the chest or head.* Also, I guessed the cult probably could not afford good bullets, hollow points, so they probably had only solid bullets. The shells would be probably .30 caliber. I contemplated the effects of being shot with

---

24. See Hebrews 2:14–15.

such bullets. They would enter very hotly and quickly without ricocheting in my body too badly and would not blow big holes going out. These were some ideas I pondered!

Supposing I had invited *you* onto that platform in Kenya, would you have hesitated to go? Your answer to that and similar questions must always be another question: *What is God saying to me?* Your decision path needs to begin first with God. What does He want you to do? When you know that, you can confidently obey Him without any fear. You see, many people hide for good reasons. If they have not heard from God about what to do in threatening environments, then fear is their only option. They *should* be afraid, if they are not serving God and are questioning whether He is on their sides!

After seeing the Kenyan guard with his big shield, armor, and machine gun, our mission team listened as I listed their two choices: Stay or go and possibly get shot. *Gulp!*

Then our team member returned from driving to the crusade grounds where the cult had destroyed our car. He had glass in his hair as he explained how the cult had beaten the car and had performed animal sacrifices across our platform. "Blood and pig entrails are everywhere!" he said. "They burned one side of the platform with their sacrifices, and they're planning to shoot us at 6:00! I heard them! They told me! So I guess you will cancel the crusade," he said to me.

"Well, I prayed," I answered. "We will go ahead with the crusade."

He quickly replied that he preferred to remain in the hotel to pray. Later, I thought his prayers were probably one of the reasons we lived! You see, the body of Christ needs each of us to do what God instructs us.

Some members of our mission team finally decided to accompany me to the crusade, believing that God's will would be done. They each said, "I am with you according to what God said, so it's okay." I needed people connected with my heart on that trip. My team stood with me, willing to risk their lives to increase the kingdom of God.

After determining who would go and who would stay to pray, the next obstacle I faced was that many of the original participants quit. Of all the musicians we had scheduled for the crusade, only a drummer came. Interpreter after interpreter also cancelled. Finally, one of the younger, zealous nationals agreed to interpret for me.

As I walked onto the platform, I saw lots of blood on the floor from the animals the cult had sacrificed. I walked across that sticky mess, wondering if I wanted to continue the crusade. Praying in the Holy Spirit, I then looked at the audience and saw many people with guns. Despite the circumstances, I launched the crusade meeting under God's direction. Those who went with me were under and behind the platform, praying. On the platform were my interpreter and me!

Staring at the gunmen, I boldly declared that night, "No man called of God will die by an assassin's bullet! Pull the trigger now if you can!" That is how God had instructed me to open the crusade.

However, my interpreter, now totally silent, was too scared to speak! I quickly whispered to him, "What's wrong with you?" We privately conversed on the platform for a few minutes as I convinced him to interpret my challenge. Meanwhile, a thousand armed cult members stood on the crusade grounds with several thousand onlookers behind them. Notice, they were *behind* the cult members. The Christians and others were watching to see if we died. That's part of the watch-and-see crowd we discussed earlier!

After a while, and after moving quite a distance away from me to avoid bullets, the interpreter finally spoke my piercing words in Swahili! A deafening silence immediately followed. The tension in the atmosphere built to a crescendo as everyone waited for the crack of the first gunshot. If you have ever heard an automatic machine gun fire, you will never forget that searing sound. We all waited for that crack in the atmosphere, but there was no sound.

Although this was the beginning of the meeting and I had not preached yet, it was a great time for an altar call! I simply announced to the crowd, "The power of God resident within me is greater than the fear and power of the devil in you. Today you must repent and give your life to Jesus!" Suddenly cult members began rushing to the platform to give their hearts to Jesus and denounce their involvement with the cult. Then the police arrested and disarmed the rest of their group that night.

The next day, Kenyan President Daniel arap Moi heard of this and personally led an entourage to arrest the leaders of the Anti-Christ Cult. He signed a declaration that abolished the cult in the entire nation. On the first night of our crusade, the crowd was very small. However, the next night, the audience grew to about fifty thousand because the armed cult members were gone and people had heard reports of what had happened. God moved mightily during that crusade.

Charisma magazine and newspapers throughout Nairobi, Kenya, carried the chilling and remarkable news. As I recall, they wrote articles with headlines such as "Death Threats Don't Stop Whetstone"[25] and "Anti-Christ Cult Shut Down by Preacher Standing in Defiance of a Bullet."

Confront and Conquer Fear with Confidence

That day at the crusade, we broke the antichrist spirit as the cult disbanded in the entire nation of Kenya. However, it did not shut down without confrontation. The Bible says, *"A wise man attacks the city of the mighty and pulls down the stronghold in which they trust"* (Proverbs 21:22 NIV). This verse reveals a spiritual principle, one that will cause you to become such an effective conqueror that the enemy cannot touch you. It shows that a wise man is active; he ascends above the enemy's trusted stronghold and successfully assaults it. Similarly, the wise, fearless Christian strikes the devil's confidence and pulls it down, destroying his enemy's strength.

That is what we had to do in Kenya. We had to confront the spirits of fear and the antichrist in that atmosphere to pull down their strongholds. I could not go to the platform apologizing for the Gospel. Instead, I had to deal directly with the cult's death threat. As Christians, we must do God's work under

> Confront the enemy's strongholds.

all conditions, fearlessly and boldly, regardless of the obstacles or resistance against us. When the devil threatens and attacks, we must confront him with confidence. God has called us to defeat darkness! We are to conquer the enemy!

Confrontation can occur in any arena of life, not only on a crusade platform in Kenya. It can be in your home. It can be in dealing with drug or

25. "Death Threats Don't Stop Whetstone," Charisma & Christian Life, June 1990, p. 17.

alcohol addiction, sexual abuse, wrong relationships, rebellious children, or other areas. You must realize that, as a Christian, the most significant areas of your life will involve confrontation. There is no doubt that you will face fear.

Whether you cower or confront fear with confidence to follow God's plan will determine your level of fulfillment and spiritual growth. It is your degree of confidence in God that determines your response to fears. Jonathan knew, as I do, that when God is in charge, His people can go gallantly into battle to conquer the enemy. In God's power, we can squarely confront fear and our enemies. God desires that we believe in Him and be confident of the victory that comes with serving Him.

Step out of Fear Today

I encourage you to connect with those who are valiant in faith as Jonathan's armorbearer did. Declare to them, "I am with you according to your heart." Allow the Holy Spirit to knit your soul with other divinely tested Christians as He did with Jonathan and David.

While connecting with valiant people, be sure to recognize the situations and relationships from which the Holy Spirit is directing you to disconnect. If God wants you to free yourself from certain involvements or people, you must not fear hurting others, being ostracized, or being judged as politically incorrect. You can allow such hostility to frighten you, or you can confront it, remaining undaunted and loyal to God's work. Choosing the latter will enable you to bring down the works of the enemy.

You see, the devil tries to use fear to keep you bound in those situations. Boldly disconnect yourself from all people who do not anchor themselves in God's design. Realign yourself with God and His faithful workers. Otherwise, you will not walk in victory. You will not have the boldness to obey God as I did at the Kenyan crusade when He instructed me to confront my enemies, saying, "Pull the trigger, if you can!"

Today step out of fear by opening your heart to Jesus. The devil tempted Him, yet He lived without sin. *"For we have not an high priest which cannot be touched with the feeling of our infirmities; but was in all points tempted like as we are, yet without sin"* (Hebrews 4:15 KJV). Jesus squarely confronted the fear of death and did not bow. He conquered all fears and did not compromise with any operation of darkness.

Ask the Holy Spirit to knit you with Jesus, so the Son of God, who loves you, will live in and through your life. When you do this, no longer will you live in your own ability or faith. Instead, you will identify with how Jesus would walk in your shoes. You will allow His power and wisdom to flow through you. The apostle Paul declared:

I have been crucified with Christ; it is no longer I who live, but Christ lives in me; and the life which I now live in the flesh I live by faith in the Son of God, who loved me and gave Himself for me. (Galatians 2:20)

When you allow Jesus to live in you, you will know how to handle your job, your family, members of His body, and every area of life. You will do exploits for the kingdom of God!

I believe that your spirit knows how to hook up with fellow believers in God's work. You see, if you are a Christian, your spirit knows no limitation; your faith knows no failure; and your vision lacks no resources. Only fear can hold you back. If you start associating with the Sauls of this world, their fears will sow limitation, failure, and lack into your heart. Decide to break away from the complacency and fear of others. Do it today. Deal with it now.

The Bible promises that signs follow the Word of God:

[The disciples] *went out and preached everywhere, the Lord working with them and confirming the word through the accompanying signs. Amen.*
(Mark 16:20)

This means you can expect evidence of the power of the Word, which you have read in these pages. Trust God that His Spirit will infuse you with bold faith, so you can break through all negativity, doubt, unbelief, and fear. The Word will liberate your heart. You will be free. I encourage you to pray this now:

Dear God of heaven, I recognize that my life is not here simply by chance but by divine appointment. I commit my destiny to You,

Father. Thank You for giving this opportunity to me to deal with certain areas in my life. Help me to use it to become qualified, as Jonathan and his armorbearer, so I can say to my dedicated brothers and sisters in Christ, "I am with you according to your heart, and, Lord, I am with You according to Your heart!"

Father, my passion is for Jesus to live His life through me, so I will not live by my own ability and faith. Jesus, let me be Your hands and feet in this world. Help me to be a mouthpiece for You to the lost and hurting.

Lord, help me to be like Jonathan and David as they valiantly ran into their conflicts to prevail. I do not want to hang back from my battles, hiding with fearful, doubting, depressed, or negative people. Help me to abort all fear-inducing conversations, relationships, thoughts, and actions. Lord, strengthen me, so I will not compromise but live as more than a conqueror. When I disconnect, help me not to fear the rejection of others or their agendas. Today, in Jesus' name, I break free from the false safety zone of fear and turn to the valiant zone of faith! In Jesus' name, Amen.

Now declare the following to your spiritual enemies:

To fear, I say, "You have no rights in my life because I am God's child! This day, I declare fear must bow. In Jesus' name, I am free from its bondage."

Finish with this prayer:

Father, thank You for helping me to break through these barriers of fear and for showing me how to remove my secret motivations of harboring fear. Thank You for moving me from the setbacks of the past to a future of exploits for You! Today, I am coming out from my cave of hiding and shedding the grave clothes of fear. From this day forth, I live as more than a conqueror for You in the valiant zone of faith. In Jesus' name, Amen.

CHAPTER NINE

BE BOLD AND FEARLESS FOR GOD

Examining the lives of ordinary people in the Bible and today, we have seen in this book how many of God's people have stepped over major thresholds of fear to accomplish great feats. Conquering their fears catapulted them into the realm of the supernatural. I pray that somewhere throughout these pages, you have made fear bow in your life!

It is critical that you become free from fear not just for your benefit, but mainly to fulfill God's will in the earth! At this time, He is calling you to be bold and fearless as you face uncertainty and various physical and spiritual conflicts. You see, God has purposed that you would become free from fear and that your freedom would liberate others!

The Cause Worth Fighting

Throughout history, God's leaders have seen a cause worth fighting for. You have one, too. Remember, as we studied earlier, God chose you before the foundation of the world. He set you on a course that caused you to be on earth at this specific time. You are here for such a time as this. The Omnipotent One, your heavenly Father, has empowered you to do what no one else can do. You have a unique contribution to this generation. The book of Ephesians says, "*But to each one of us grace was given according to the measure of Christ's gift*" (Ephesians 4:7).

God has dispensed to you the ability to operate in His power through the Holy Spirit. It is the Spirit of God who will cause you to win against the enemy. As we studied earlier, you do not have to depend on your education, knowledge, natural abilities, or history of being brave and strong. God sees more in you than you suspect because He knows what *He* deposited within you, "*the measure of Christ's gift.*" You are a masterpiece of God! The Bible teaches: "*For we are God's workmanship, created in Christ Jesus to do good works, which God prepared in advance for us to do*" (Ephesians 2:10 NIV).

The works you are to do are not ordinary. They are God-ordained exploits, which He will work through you. This may be unfamiliar territory to you because you will not be able to do these assignments in your own strength. When you step into these divine works, you will become extremely vulnerable. You will have to depend on God because He will be working through you.

The Spirit of God has a very peculiar way of extracting what He has deposited in you. One of the ways He does this is by placing you into environments that require you to take extraordinary steps to stand in faith and valor. That is how God operated with Abraham, Moses, Jonathan and David, Joshua, and so many others whose stories are recorded in God's Word. As He acted in the past, God continues to operate with every one of His children today. He will do the same with you.

Prove God's Dominion

You see, God desires to prove to you who He is. Moreover, He wants to prove who He is to the world, whom He longs to set free through *you!* It does not matter how difficult the circumstances are. It matters only how focused and free you are! God has purposed for you to show this world a new way of living. He has made you for signs and wonders to prove who He is, not for fear and holding back His spiritual gifts in you. No matter how challenging the situation, God will see you through it.

When you obey God, your flesh may not enjoy the experience or the trials. However, the Bible declares:

Beloved, do not think it strange concerning the fiery trial which is to try you, as though some strange thing happened to you; but rejoice to the extent that you partake of Christ's sufferings, that when His glory is revealed, you may also be glad with exceeding joy. (1 Peter 4:12–13)

You see, God wants the glory, and He receives it when you successfully walk through fiery trials. The proof of Christ in you comes out in hostile environments. Then God shows Himself as God because you cannot handle the circumstances alone. Only He can do it.

Many of us spend our entire lives struggling to be in control of our circumstances. We do not want to be in difficult situations or trials that are bigger than we are. Instead, we carefully arrange our environments so that we can be in charge. However, the best place to be is *not* in control. We need to be where God is in control and where we are powerless in our natural abilities to affect change. Then God can prove who He is!

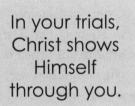

In your trials, Christ shows Himself through you.

You might be asking yourself, *Well, what will that do for me?*

It will give you new steps to take to bring God's influence on the scene. Walking fearlessly with God will shock and thrill you to no end! When you allow God to be in charge, your life will be so exciting, you will hardly be able to stand it! I wake up early every day, ecstatic to be alive and serving God at this time in history. Do you realize this is one of the most exciting times on the earth? It is exhilarating to know that the demand of God's nature in us is at hand.

A Great Awakening

This is a unique time, because a large stirring of faith began to occur after the terrorist attacks in the United States in 2001. People began to look for something greater than themselves because they came to the end of their strength and power. They were helpless. Not only did these events lead to the tragic death and injury of thousands, but the attacks also sparked the realization that terrorists can strike anywhere at any moment in any way. The U.S. economy plunged, stocks plummeted, and companies announced layoffs. People began to fear and fall into confusion.

As the world looks at the shocking events of our day, they cower in fear. However, we do not have to fear because we believe a different report: the Good News. Do you see this as a great time to spread the Gospel and to prove God not only in your life but in others' lives? I see it as the greatest time of spiritual harvest in our generation. People are more open to having an experience with God than I have ever known. Let's focus on bringing the kingdom of God into this earth during this time.

It is critical for Christians to be about their Father's work because the cults also will have one of their greatest influences during this time. Instability is the best time to bring converts to any faith, including false religions such as Islam, Hare Krishna, and Eastern philosophies. At such times, people look for any type of belief to quiet their fears. One of the tragedies is that they may hook up to the wrong ones. Therefore, you and I have a great responsibility. Knowing people's hearts are open, we must be the ones to plant the right seeds in those lives.

> Let God use what He has placed inside you.

Someone will answer the questions and calm the fears of the people around you. That someone needs to be *you*, because *you* have the *true* answers. God has deposited Truth into your life. As we discussed, giving those answers will move you into new actions in new environments, which may not be comfortable. However, that is how to use the gift of God's nature inside your life to meet the demand. Allowing God to extract what He has placed in you is the most rewarding thing you can do.

What Has God Deposited in You for this Time?

The point comes down to you. What has God deposited in you? What do you have that is in demand right now? What does God want to come from you at this time? Where is it? How does it function? Whatever it is, God will receive the glory in it when He shows Himself strong through you.

At first, you may not recognize what God has placed inside you, but He will reveal it to you if you seek Him. When He speaks to you to act, you must obey. Believing Him is not enough. You must put action to your faith. The Bible explains: *"For as the body without the spirit is dead, so faith without works is dead also"* (James 2:26). The Christian walk is not a passive existence. Remember, God preordained the works you are to do, and through your actions, He will undeniably prove Himself as God.

Be Accountable to God

The Bible explains that each of us will give an account to God for our responses regarding what He has deposited in us. Regardless of whether we live or die, we must obey Him and be wise stewards of His gifts within us. As the apostle Paul wrote,

> *None of us lives to himself, and no one dies to himself. For if we live, we live to the Lord; and if we die, we die to the Lord. Therefore, whether we live or die, we are the Lord's.* (Romans 14:7–8)

In these verses, Paul summed up what a Christian's attitude ought to be, and in many places in the New Testament we see that Paul lived out this belief. He did not concern himself with dying. Instead, he chose to obey God at all costs because he belonged to the Lord. Clearly, people such as Jonathan and David and Joshua chose the same.

Paul continued:

> *But why do you judge your brother? Or why do you show contempt for your brother? For we shall all stand before the judgment seat of Christ. For it is written: "As I live, says the Lord, every knee shall bow to Me, and every tongue shall confess to God." So then each of us shall give account of himself to God.* (verses 10–12)

Because you will give an account to God, you do not have the option of being fearful, negative, confused, or doubtful. That is where the world lives, but not you. God has called you to live on a plane that surpasses all worldly reactions and causes you to release that which He has deposited within you. As a Christian, you have no other choice.

How Can You Do This?

By now, you probably have the picture of your responsibility as a child of God. You are first to subdue your own human mind-set by walking with God, and then you are to bring others into that experience with the Lord. Now, exactly how can you fulfill what God has called you to do? Below are several ways to do this at our present time in history.

Turn (Repent) and Focus on God's Word

As we discussed earlier, you should not give attention to fear, confusion, doubt, unbelief, torment, condemnation, or accusation. Do not meditate on this type of negative communication. Instead, turn from it. This does not require a great mind. If I can do it, you can do it! Turn from it to focus on God's Word. Doing this is repenting! To repent means simply to turn around to go the other way. When you turn from the influence to the answer, you become free from the control of that influence.

> Our faith-walk will encourage others.

Certainly, people will continue to carry out destructive acts, and other fearful events will happen in our lifetimes. However, our responsibility is not to be paranoid. We are to walk in faith, not fear. Then we can help revive others. However, we will be unable to do this unless we first remove the enemy's influence in our lives and allow God's nature to be resident, having full sway in us.

Watch and Pray, Then Minister

This is a sobering time in history. The age-old Bible still applies to us today when it says, *"But the end of all things is at hand; therefore be serious and watchful in your prayers"* (1 Peter 4:7).

We are to watch in prayer. Here Peter did not mean to check out our environment only with our natural eyes to see what is happening. No, he was warning us to have our wits attuned and our prayer lives focused. This is how we will truly see what is happening in the spiritual realm during this end time. Our ability to see spiritually is only as good as our ability to see what God is saying to us through prayer.

Peter wrote further:

And above all things have fervent love for one another, for "love will cover a multitude of sins." Be hospitable to one another without grumbling. As each one has received a gift, minister it to one another, as good stewards of the manifold grace of God. If anyone speaks, let him speak as the oracles of God. If anyone ministers, let him do it as with the ability which God supplies, that in all things God may be glorified through Jesus Christ, to whom belong the glory and the dominion forever and ever. Amen. (1 Peter 4:8–11)

Notice in the last verse above, Peter was instructing the Lord's people to speak and minister as God gave the ability to them. What does it say would be the result if they did this? God would have the glory and dominion. Now, what is dominion? It is a territory of rule. This verse is clearly telling us that God will show His authority in this territory of rule through His people. That's you!

Let Peter's words speak to you today. They identify the time you are in as the end days. They advise you to be sober, vigilant, and clear in your mind, staying focused in prayer. That is the only way you will know what to do. They remind you that you will not overcome conflict by your natural abilities but as God enables you.

Peter also explained that this is a spiritual combat, not a natural one. He said that you are a steward of what God has deposited in your life for these times, and you need to minister it to others on a supernatural plane. So take that gift and give it to others, using your faith to step from the natural into the unseen, spiritual arena. Then God will have all glory and dominion forever and ever. Hallelujah!

Speak the Word

Peter said we should *"speak as the oracles of God"* (1 Peter 4:11). The *New International Version* of the Bible translates this as *"speaking the very words of*

God." What does this mean? It means that we are to speak the written Word of God—the Bible. As God's Word says, *"Since we have the same spirit of faith, according to what is written, 'I believed and therefore I spoke,' we also believe and therefore speak"* (2 Corinthians 4:13).

Find verses dealing with the situation you and others face, and then speak those words aloud. For example, the Bible tells us what we are to do in times of wars and rumors of wars: *"And you will hear of wars and rumors of wars. See that you are not troubled; for all these things must come to pass, but the end is not yet"* (Matthew 24:6). We are not to be troubled.

Therefore, if people are worried, you will have a Word in season to revive the weary. God's Word promises:

> *The Lord God hath given me the tongue of the learned, that I should know how to speak a word in season to him that is weary: he wakeneth [me] morning by morning, he wakeneth mine ear to hear as the learned.*
>
> (Isaiah 50:4 KJV)

Your words carry far more weight now than ever before! Many people today are talking only about the fearful events they have been seeing, but God has called you to speak what they cannot see. He has given you an avenue into their hearts, but it is up to you to use it.

Remember, your words have great power. They can do one of two things:

+ Invoke God's purposes and promises to bring them into manifestation, or
+ Actually abort God's purpose and promises.

The book of James says regarding the power of our tongues,

> *We all stumble in many ways. If anyone is never at fault in what he says, he is a perfect man, able to keep his whole body in check. When we put bits into the mouths of horses to make them obey us, we can turn the whole animal. Or take ships as an example. Although they are so large and are driven by strong winds, they are steered by a very small rudder wherever the pilot wants to go. Likewise the tongue is a small part of the body, but it makes great boasts. Consider what a great forest is set on fire by a small spark. The tongue also is a fire, a world of evil among the parts of the body. It*

corrupts the whole person, sets the whole course of his life on fire, and is itself
set on fire by hell.   (James 3:2–6 NIV)

With the words of your mouth, you can direct
lives to go in the right direction. Therefore, I urge
you to speak God's Word into the lives of people
around you to combat the devil's attacks. When you
do, your words—God's Word—will become the
avenue by which God fulfills His promises to them.

> **Speak the Word and feast on it.**

This is also true in your own life. I cannot emphasize enough how critical
it is that you align your words with God's. The Bible teaches:

From the fruit of his mouth a man's stomach is filled; with the harvest from
his lips he is satisfied. The tongue has the power of life and death, and those
who love it will eat its fruit.   (Proverbs 18:20–21 NIV)

What are *you* having for your spiritual dinner tonight? Wouldn't you like it
to be a nice plate of words you really want to eat? Then you can enjoy the benefit
of those words manifesting in your life. Make your spiritual meals feasts on the
Word of God. The Bible is not for you simply to read; no, you are to speak it also.

Let God's Word establish His defenses in your life and the lives of those
around you so that He can fulfill His promises to His people. Remember,
Jesus said, "*When you pray, say: Our Father in heaven, hallowed be Your name.*
Your kingdom come. Your will be done on earth as it is in heaven" (Luke 11:2).

When you pray, God wants you to establish His kingdom of heaven,
which is His will, on earth. Praying His Word is one way to do this.

God is calling upon you to pray things into existence that do not yet appear.
If you depend upon yourself to accomplish them, great fear will come into your
life. However, you must remember that if God said it, He is the One responsible to make it happen. If it does not manifest, go back to check that God really
said it. If He did, then it *will* occur. All creation will work together with Him to
fulfill His will.[26] Be sure not to utter fear-propelled prayer, because fear is not
an instrument of God. It has no place in the kingdom of heaven.

---

26. See Romans 8:18–22 and Ephesians 1:9–12.

Pray Psalm 91

An excellent and easy example of how to pray the Word of God is to use Psalm 91. All around the world, people continually confess and decree this psalm aloud over their lives. You, too, need to make this a habit, if you have not already done so. In fact, you should regularly take time to focus on what God has promised in His Word and commit yourself to seeing it manifested.

The following is how to personalize God's Word using Psalm 91 as an example:

I dwell in Your secret place, Most High God. I abide under Your shadow, almighty Lord. I say You are my refuge and fortress, my God. I trust in You. Surely, You deliver me from the snare of the fowler and from the noisome pestilence. You cover me with Your feathers, and under Your wings I trust. Your truth is my shield and buckler (defense and protection).

You cause me not to be afraid of the terror by night, the arrow that flies by day, the pestilence that walks in darkness, nor the destruction that wastes at noonday. A thousand may fall at my side and ten thousand at my right hand, but I thank You that it is not coming near me. Only with my eyes shall I see the reward of the wicked.

Because I have made You my habitation (dwelling place), O Lord the Most High God, who is my refuge, no evil shall befall me, neither shall any plague come near my building.

For, God, You have given Your angels charge over me, to keep me in all my ways. They bear me up in their hands, lest I dash even my foot against a stone. Oh, God, I thank You that I tread upon the lion and adder. The young lion and dragon (every opposition) I trample under my feet.

God, You said that because I have set my love upon You, You deliver me. You set me on high (as You put me in Christ) because I have known Your name. You said that I call upon You, and You answer me. (I know that You have a great answer, God!) I thank You that You promised to be with me in trouble, to deliver me, and to honor me. You said with long life You will satisfy me. Every day of my life, You will show Your salvation to me.

Now, spend a moment right now thanking God for who He is to you today. Thank Him for who He is to you in the midst of a world of confusion and fear. Thank Him for who He is to you in the

> Thank God for who He is.

oppression and concerns of your life. Stop to thank Him for being your supply and protection every day of your life. Now, encourage others to do the same.

Do Not Grow Weary and Faint

You must not ever grow weary and faint because of circumstances around you. Do you realize that as soon as you faint in your mind or spirit, you relinquish the authority of making your own conscionable decisions? You surrender to the leadership of another, because fainting people can be carried anywhere, even against their desires. Remember, as we discussed earlier, the military strategist Carl von Clausewitz defined *war* as "an act of violence intended to compel our opponent to fulfill our will."[27] When you faint, you lose the war, because you lose the ability to function, thus giving your enemy power over you. However, a person in control of his or her faculties decides what to do next. God wants you to have that type of a sobriety so that you can decide to exercise His power within you at all times.

Pray with Others

In times of crisis or fear, people are often more open to prayer. This is a powerful tool God has given to us to dissipate worries and fears. Resistance to prayer is likely to be low at such times in your workplace, school, unsaved relatives' homes, and other areas where it was previously frowned upon. If you approach it wisely, people may even invite you to pray.

You can quote 1 Timothy 2:8, saying, "*I want men everywhere to lift up holy hands in prayer, without anger or disputing*" (1 Timothy 2:8 NIV). Here God says to pray "*everywhere*." You can take this verse, for example, to your supervisor at work or the principal at your school, saying, "God wants '*men everywhere*' to pray. I am here. This place is included in '*everywhere*.' Therefore, to obey God, we need to pray here!" That is your authority to pray where you work, at school, and everywhere. There is nowhere you are unable to pray! Just remember to do it on your time, not that of your employer.

---

27. Clausewitz, p. 101.

You may have to break through the fearsome barrier of communicating with others about the need to pray. Maybe you will need to conquer the obstacle of a company policy. It may be uncomfortable, but you must do it. For example, you can say to your supervisor, "At lunch I would like to have half of the lunch time during which people can come to pray, and I would lead a prayer meeting. I am willing to make fliers at my own expense and on my own time to pass out to all the people in our business here. How about it? Is this all right with you?"

You can also say that the President continually asks all of us to pray for the safety of our nation, and you simply want to honor the request of the President of the United States. How can they refute that? They liked it when many people, especially ladies, took seriously the President's plea for us to go shopping to help the economy after the attacks on September 11, 2001!

Another idea is to quote 1 Timothy 2:1–2, which says:

> *Therefore I exhort first of all that supplications, prayers, intercessions, and giving of thanks be made for all men, for kings and all who are in authority, that we may lead a quiet and peaceable life in all godliness and reverence.*

Probably not one person will disagree with that. It is obvious that the President and all in authority need prayer. Also, no one wants to live in fear and tyranny but in peace and quiet. Simply say you want to pray for the leadership of our country and for peace in our nation.

> **Fears can open people's hearts to their need of God.**

Then, when you pray in your group, begin your prayer as you promised, whether it is for safety or peace in our nation, or for all those in authority. Next, after you have determined what people are worried about, pray God's Word in those areas of personal concern. For example, if any of the people there have family members in the Armed Forces, let them know they have the right to commit their family members into the Lord's hands to keep them. Then pray to Your Savior who does not lose wars. If the people are worried about losing their jobs or if they have sick family members, pray the Word of God with them in those areas. If young people are concerned about crazed fellow students attacking them on their campuses, pray for their safety and the exposing of any evil plots against the schools.

As people struggle with challenges, talk to them about how their fears have opened their hearts to believe in God. Now is the time for people to come to grips with their mortality and lack of control over their environments. This is the time to realize that an unseen enemy, without a second thought, can unexpectedly kill the innocent. It is time to understand that stability in any area of life can crack at any moment. As people dwell on the negative they are hearing, you can use that information to open a door of faith into their hearts to calm their fear and silence its influence. Then lead them to Christ.

Reap the Harvest

Do you feel convicted that the people in your workplace, school, or family are ready for salvation? Then lead them to Christ! Maybe no one else except you can do it. I will not be going there tomorrow, but you will. I cannot speak to the people you can talk to. I cannot get to them during lunch in your workplace, school, or home. I cannot talk to your community as you can. I do not know your family as you do. They want to know what is next. Tell them that whatever happens, they can be secure in Jesus. This is your chance.

Now, if you do not know how to lead people to the Lord, refer to Appendix A of this book. Also, you may purchase my book *The Victorious Walk*. You can simply read it to them because it takes you through the prayer of salvation. It also lists Scripture verses and other prayers to comfort people in their areas of torment. It is very easy to use. Many other tools are available to help you pray for people. You can find them at a Christian bookstore or maybe at your church.

Find ways to communicate the gospel that minimize people's defenses and create inroads into their hearts and lives. That's what we need to look for, not ways to polarize and alienate unbelievers.

This reminds me of a ministry trip to Nigeria I took some years ago with Archbishop Benson Idahosa.[28] It was during a period of violent clashes in North Nigeria between Christians and Muslims. Hundreds of killings had taken place between these religious groups in the cities of Jos and Kaduna. Civil tension was very high. Because of the riots and murders, the government

---

28. Archbishop Benson Idahosa (1938–1998) founded Church of God Mission International, Inc. and Idahosa World Outreach in Benin City, Nigeria. Outreaches of this multifaceted ministry include Benson Idahosa University, All Nations for Christ Bible Institute International, and Faith Medical Complex. For further information about this continuing ministry, visit their web site at cgmonline.org.

even banned public preaching and open-air crusades for a time. However, after they lifted the ban, we were the first to do a crusade in that Muslim sector.

Great fear permeated the area, and people were reluctant to attend our services. A strong probability existed that someone would try to prove the Muslim faith was still worth killing for. The police could not protect anyone, so Archbishop Idahosa and I agreed in prayer that God was bigger than our circumstances and we would not die at this event. You see, we believed the people were worth saving, and God's authority demands that His Word be publicly declared regardless of the obstacles. As we walked onto the crusade grounds to preach that day, the tension was high. We were about to preach Jesus to a crowd filled with Muslims in an unstable environment! Even the air seemed heavy.

What happened next was very exciting. The archbishop immediately opened a book and quoted a section. Incredibly, it was the Koran, the Islamic bible! "From your prophet Mohammed," Archbishop Idahosa announced, "this book states Jesus is a true prophet, so you should listen to him." He closed the Koran and picked up the Christian Bible, boldly declaring, "I'm carrying out the words of Mohammed!" He went on to preach the gospel. Do you realize what he did? He nullified all arguments, silenced all prejudice, and ended all polarity. It was awesome!

> **Ask God how you can minimize people's defenses.**

That day, Archbishop Idahosa quoted several passages, including this one from Sura 19:31–32, 34, which the Koran attributes to Jesus:

Lo, I am God's servant; God has given me the Book, and made me a Prophet. Blessed He has made me, wherever I may be; and He has enjoined me to pray, and to give the alms, so long as I live....Peace be upon me, the day I was born, and the day I die, and the day I am raised up alive![29]

Following these words is this verse in Sura 19:35: "That is Jesus, son of Mary, in word of truth, concerning which they are doubting."[30]

---

29. On this occasion, Archbishop Benson Idahosa quoted the following passages from the Koran: Sura 3:5; Sura 19:41, 47; Sura 19:30–40; Suratul Nisan 4:171; and Suratul Nisan 4:170. Other references that are useful in ministering to Muslims include Sura 19:16–29 and Sura 43:63.

30. *The Koran Interpreted*, trans. Arthur J. Arberry (New York: Collier Books, Macmillan, 1955), p. 333.

This is one way to minister to Muslims. Ask God to reveal other ways to minimize people's defenses, so you can pray with them. Whatever God shows you to do, do it. I believe at this time that He wants to use you in greater ways than ever before. Do not back down from His plan. Step into it.

Now is God's time for you. The answers to your prayers are in front of you. The salvation of some of your family, friends, and coworkers is only a prayer away. Ask God for wisdom, and He will give it to you. Financial break-throughs are coming. Some are only a decision away. People need answers to prayers, and you know the God who has the answers!

We need to wake up to realize this is a great time of harvest. Jesus said,

> *Do you not say, "There are still four months and then comes the harvest"? Behold, I say to you, lift up your eyes and look at the fields, for they are already white for harvest!* (John 4:35)

> *The harvest truly is plentiful, but the laborers are few. Therefore pray the Lord of the harvest to send out laborers into His harvest.* (Matthew 9:37–38)

This is the time to harvest people for God, regardless of any apparent challenges. Do you realize that the enemy stands the strongest against you at harvest time? Fear and confusion rise. Threatening environmental conditions tempt you to think you will lose your crop. However, as a harvester, you should not fix your eyes on the circumstances around you. Instead, focus on the responsibility that God has set before you. Bring people to Christ. Give them the comfort and strength of prayer and the Word of God, for when you speak God's Word to people, the anointing (or power of God) on it brings them directly to God Himself. Then He can battle on their behalf.

Boldly walk through the open doors of evangelism in your environment, and do not let them shut again. Inroads for prayer exist all around you. If you do not act when it is your time, you will miss your harvest. Know that you are an instrument of righteousness in the hands of almighty God. You are His voice of

Let faith rise in your heart.

authority against the devil's curse and bondage in your community. Live as the instrument of triumph God has already made you!

Go for It!

Today, those who are putting a demand on God's nature within them and responding to the Lord are bringing great transformation in this world. I believe what God has deposited within you is for this time in history. You must release it regardless of the cost. Remember, if you are a Christian, whether you live or die, you are God's. Go for it, because you may not have a better opportunity in your lifetime. The course of future events may depend on you!

You are living in a time that God has specifically hewn from the annals of eternity. Today, like no other day, faith must rise in your heart to fulfill His plan for your life. Do not allow the intimidation and restrictions of fear to stay in your life. It is time to make fear bow!

Do not think of yourself as an insignificant, powerless individual. My friend, that is not true. It is time to see yourself not as a victim but as a valiant hero for God. He has commissioned you as a bold, fearless combatant against all the forces of darkness! The Spirit of the living God has empowered you to fulfill His purposes. Break every grip of fear and torment that the enemy has launched against your life, family, ministry, city, country, and God's dreams in your heart. Only then can you move in the purpose He has for your life.

The world needs what God has hidden in you. Now is the time to let it out! Nothing can stop you, except fear itself, so make fear bow!

Prayers to Freedom and Fulfillment

As we close this book, I encourage you to pray the following prayers from your heart:

Prayer to Release God's Deposit within You

Father, I take a stand today, believing that You have called and placed me on this earth for such a time as this. I recognize that before the foundations of this world, You designed me to be here at this time. For Your eternal purposes, You deposited within me a measure of Your anointing. Help me to use that gift within me to increase my influence for Your kingdom. I look to You, God, for the validation, demonstration, and manifestation of all You have placed within me.

Spirit of the living God, You have empowered me and launched me from the natural arena into the supernatural realm. Thank You that all Your promises are "Yes and Amen"[31] to me. In Jesus' name, Amen.

Prayer for the Harvesters

Father, You are the Lord of the Harvest. I ask You to open the eyes of all Your people, including me, to see Your harvest and reap it. I lift before You the people in my family, school, workplace, community, nation, and the world. Help me to see the harvest on my doorstep.

Father, I ask You to cause every one of Your harvesters to be bold and effective in our communications. Put stout and convicted hearts in us to speak Your Word in season to revive the weary, lift burdens, and break yokes. God, I pray that the anointing of Your Spirit within Your children permeates, penetrates, and liberates those around us. Cause Your people to make a difference in the darkness surrounding us. God, I pray that we, as Your harvesters, will not simply exist on this earth but will fulfill Your purposes.

Help us to know how to release from within ourselves the power of the One who raised Jesus from the dead. Father, let Your harvesters stand out as shining stars for all to see who You are. Help us to grasp the revelation that You live in us and we live in You. Therefore, wherever we go, You go. Wherever we go, the Deliverer goes. Wherever we go, the Healer goes. Wherever we go, salvation goes. Wherever we go, freedom goes. Wherever we go, financial breakthroughs go. Wherever we go, miracles go. Father, help us to minister who You are to this lost and hurting world, so we can reap it for You! In Jesus' name, Amen.

---

31. See 2 Corinthians 1:20.

Prayer for the Church to Stand against the Enemy

Father, we stand as one nation under God. Also, Your people stand as Your kingdom in this earth, and nothing can overthrow it. I decree that what the enemy has intended for harm, God is turning around for good. In Jesus' name, I sever the enemy's power in our country and on God's people. Lord, You said the gates of hell will not prevail against Your church.[32] I pray for bold conviction to kick open the gates that have bound the captives. Father, empower Your children to release the burdens that have crippled and weighed people down. Thank You for honoring and performing Your Word through Your church.

Holy Spirit of God, show Yourself strong on behalf of Your people. Cause our successes in fiery trials to prove that You keep Your promises. Thank You, Father, that You are completing the work You have begun within us.

In Jesus' name, I rebuke negativity, fear, confusion, torment, doubt, and unbelief. They have no influence on my life or on the people of the living God, who has called us into action. God, we will not cower in huddles of fear and confusion. We refuse to succumb to the limitations of human endeavor. We refuse to bow to the appearances of things. We refuse to cower in the presence of any circumstances. Father, thank You for giving to us Your authority to subdue every power that rages against us. We declare to all that withstands us that our God is our refuge and dwelling place. Nothing has the power to bind us in fear because nothing can bind God in fear. Therefore, in Jesus' name, we command fear to bow!

Prayer of Obedience

Spirit of the living God, thank You that Your perfect love casts out all fear.[33] Thank You, Jesus, for the great security of knowing You as Lord and Savior of my life. Help me not to waver in my convictions to

---

32. See Matthew 16:18.
33. See 1 John 4:18.

serve you. When you put me to the test, may I stand strong in faith and valor for You.

I am beginning to see the significance and the influence You have placed within my life. You have designed me to bring Your kingdom and will to this world. Thank You for the privilege of being on this earth as Your ambassador and speaking as an oracle of God. Help me to remember that mine are not mere human words, but transforming Words from the living God.

This day, I stand before You, Spirit of God, declaring that I yield myself to You. I yield myself to hear Your voice, know Your ways, walk in Your person, and experience Your power. Help me to fulfill all You have purposed and set before me to carry out. Help me to obey You. I will go beyond my comfort zone to make a difference for Your kingdom, not judging others. Through my life, let all around me taste of Your kingdom. May they see Your reigning glory and dominion.

Most High God, I bless and magnify Your name! I lift my voice with a shout of triumph. I praise You. In Jesus' name, Amen.

APPENDIX A

CONQUER MANKIND'S TWO GREATEST FEARS

Do you want to move into a realm of freedom in which nothing has the power to hold you back? This will happen when you conquer the two greatest fears that mankind faces: death and hell. You can settle this issue within the next couple of minutes. Then nothing will be able to hold you back when you take the following truths to heart!

First, the fear of death greatly limits many people. It affects their lives so much that they do nothing that involves risk. But life is filled with risks. You simply cannot live in this uncertain world without risk. If you try to avoid it, you will allow the fear of death to control you and cripple you. However, you do not have to live this way. The Bible says,

> *Inasmuch then as the children have partaken of flesh and blood, He Himself likewise shared in the same, that through death He might destroy him who had the power of death, that is, the devil, and release those who through fear of death were all their lifetime subject to bondage.* (Hebrews 2:14–15)

> *"Death has been swallowed up in victory. Where, O death, is your victory? Where, O death, is your sting?" The sting of death is sin….But thanks be*

to God! He gives us the victory through our Lord Jesus Christ. Therefore, my dear brothers, stand firm. Let nothing move you. Always give yourselves fully to the work of the Lord, because you know that your labor in the Lord is not in vain. (1 Corinthians 15:54–58 NIV)

Jesus has conquered death for you, so you can be free!

*For if, by the trespass of the one man [Adam], **death reigned** through that one man, how much more will those who receive God's abundant provision of grace and of the gift of righteousness **reign in life through the one man, Jesus Christ**....But where sin increased, grace increased all the more, so that, just as sin reigned in death, so also grace might reign through righteousness to bring eternal life through Jesus Christ our Lord.*

(Romans 5:17, 20–21 NIV, emphasis added)

Do you see that Jesus reversed the curse of death? Now, instead of death reigning over you, *you* can reign in *life!* Therefore, you do not need to fear death any longer. Break free from its confines today. I will show you how in a moment. When you do, you can live boldly, overcoming anything with unwavering certainty. You can fully draw upon God's grace and power by faith.

Second, the fear of hell is another major challenge for people. Supposing I went to any street where people are and asked them, "Do you have a fear of going to hell?"

The unsaved would likely respond, "No, I don't believe in it, but I'll probably go there with all my friends." Answers such as this expose the fact that people have a real fear of hell, because they are uncertain as to their eternal outcomes in life. If *you* are not sure what will happen to you after you die, you can change that right now. You must be certain where you will go. You must have this assurance *right now.* Here's how. Are you ready?

Get Your Free Gift

When Jesus Christ died on the cross and rose bodily from the grave, He fully paid for your sin and its consequences. The Bible says: *"For God so loved the world that He gave His only begotten Son, that whoever believes in Him should not perish but have everlasting life"* (John 3:16).

Since Jesus paid for your sins, you don't have to. Your salvation is His free gift. You need only to receive it. *"But as many as received Him, to them He gave the right to become children of God, to those who believe in His name"* (John 1:12). *"For by grace you have been saved through faith, and that not of yourselves; it is the gift of God, not of works, lest anyone should boast"* (Ephesians 2:8–9).

The way to receive God's gift is to believe His Word and simply receive it by prayer and by saying it with your mouth.

> *That if you confess with your mouth, "Jesus is Lord," and believe in your heart that God raised him from the dead, you will be saved. For it is with your heart that you believe and are justified, and it is with your mouth that you confess and are saved.* (Romans 10:9–10 NIV)

To do this now, pray the following prayer aloud:

Father, thank You for loving me. Thank You for giving Your Son, Jesus, to die and be raised from the dead for me. Accepting your free gift of Jesus will loose me from the fears of death and hell.

Jesus Christ, Son of God, come into my heart, forgive me of my sins, and be my Lord and Savior. Jesus, I declare that You are Lord, and that You are Lord of my life.

Thank You, Father, for the rights I now have to every benefit of Jesus' death. The blood of Jesus forgave all my sins. The blood is the danger zone for the devil because it declares that I am in right standing with God. I am a new creation. Jesus has loosed me from the grip of condemnation.

Father, this very covenant gives me the right to walk fear-free. The blood of Jesus has defeated every accusation, silenced every word of condemnation, and canceled all guilt and shame. Jesus has given victory to me over all the power of the enemy. Now, no weapon formed against me will prosper. This covenant, Jesus' blood, prevails over all. Today, I receive every benefit of Your Word in Jesus' name.

Father, thank You for Your promise of receiving the Holy Spirit. Holy Spirit of God, I am Yours. Fill me with Your very presence. By Your power, demonstrate Your awesome authority through my life. In Jesus' name, Amen.

Hallelujah, you are now born again! You have just stepped from the kingdom of Darkness into the kingdom of Light with God as your heavenly Father. As His child, you now have the authority through Jesus to make fear bow!

All believers are entitled to over seven thousand promises that God has written in His Word. That includes you! To learn about these promises, attend church regularly. Wherever you are, I encourage you to attend a local church that teaches the uncompromised Word of God—the Bible.

Daily, spend time in prayer, fellowship with the Lord, and reading the Bible. These things will help you to understand the *"new creature"* (2 Corinthians 5:17 KJV) that you have become now in Christ: *"Therefore, if anyone is in Christ, he is a new creation; old things have passed away; behold, all things have become new"* (verse 17).

Well, glory! Go ahead and shout unto the Lord with a voice of triumph! Bless Him. Now, I encourage you to follow God, serve Him with all your heart, and watch what He will do through your life.

APPENDIX B

The prayer at the end of chapter 4 is based on the following Scriptures:

John 10:1–16, 27–30; Psalm 5:8; Luke 3:4–6; Isaiah 55:12 (KJV); Psalm 23:3; 119:105 (KJV); Isaiah 48:17; Ephesians 1:3 (KJV); Genesis 39:3; Joshua 1:7; Psalm 1:3; Jeremiah 17:8; Isaiah 54:17; 2 Corinthians 10:4 (NIV); Isaiah 41:10; 59:16–17; Psalm 68:33–35; Deuteronomy 1:21; 31:1–8; Exodus 3:14–15; Isaiah 54:5; Exodus 22:22–24; Deuteronomy 10:17–18; Psalm 10:12–18; 146:9; 68:5–6; Isaiah 51:11–12; 61:1–3; Matthew 5:4; John 14:16–18; 2 Corinthians 1:3–4; Isaiah 41:10; Psalm 73:26; Philippians 4:13; Psalm 46:1–2; 31:24; 71:5; Jeremiah 17:7–8; Romans 15:13; Jeremiah 3:14; 2 Samuel 22; Psalm 144:2; 55:18; Romans 15:13, 33; Proverbs 16:7; Mark 4:39; John 14:27; 16:33; Philippians 4:7; Psalm 4:8; 16:11; 43:4; 105:43; 126:5–6; Romans 4:17; 15:13; Galatians 5:22; John 1:1–4; 4:14; 6:47–51; 11:25; 14:6; Ephesians 1:20–23; Hebrews 3:4; 1 Corinthians 15:28; Mark 9:23 (NIV); 1 Peter 2:25; 5:4; Proverbs 7:2; Matthew 19:28; 1 Corinthians 15:24–28; Genesis 17:1; 1 Corinthians 1:30; Hebrews 1:8; 7:2; Romans 5:17–21; 3:22–26; 2 Timothy 4:8; Luke 4:18; 2 Corinthians 3:17; Galatians 5:1; Exodus 17:15–16; Isaiah 11:10 (NIV); Jeremiah 23:6; Joel 2:21–29; Genesis 22:13–14; 2 Corinthians 8:9; Leviticus 20:8; Genesis 28:3–4; Psalm 111:10; Proverbs 2:1–11; 8:1–21; 9:10; Romans 12:3; Matthew 21:21–22; 2 Corinthians 4:18; Hebrews 11:1–3; Isaiah 11:16; Deuteronomy 31:8; Isaiah 52:12; 58:8; Psalm 91:7; Genesis 28:15; Exodus 3:16–17; Deuteronomy 2:7; Psalm 1:6; Jeremiah 1:12; Numbers 23:19.

GARY WHETSTONE
WORLDWIDE MINISTRIES

The Great Commission calls upon us to effect real change, to bring a light to the nations! This light is the message of Jesus Christ and God's love for the world. This is what motivates us at Gary Whetstone Worldwide Ministries. This ministry has many outreaches in which you can become involved. Below are ways you can become a light to the nations with us!

For more information, visit our web site at www.gwwm.com, Email info@ gwwm.com, call 1 (302) 324-5400, fax 1 (302) 324-5448, or write Gary Whetstone Worldwide Ministries, P.O. Box 10050, Wilmington, Deleware, 19850.

Prayer Command Centers

God has given a mandate to Dr. Gary V. Whetstone to plant Prayer Command Centers around the globe. These are simply places and times whereby Christians assemble with one or two to any number of people for prayer. Prayer Command Centers can be in houses, at workplaces, in schools, on the telephone, at any place of meeting, and through any form of communication, such as the Internet.

In these centers, people spend thirty to forty-five minutes in focused prayer once a week. The purpose is for the people of God to take responsibility in prayer to engage Jesus' authority in the earth, especially in seven key arenas of influence:

+ Yourself

+ Your family

+ Your local church: the vision, the pastor, the community, and the people of the church

+ Governments and all those in authority

+ Jesus to send laborers into His harvest fields

+ The door of utterance to open for God's Word to have its access and penetration around this globe through Prayer Command Centers, the School of Biblical Studies, all functions of GWWM, and evangelism

+ The church to cry in unison, "Come, Lord Jesus!"

Gary Whetstone Worldwide Ministries provides the tools and teaching to help establish you in exercising Jesus' authority in your Prayer Command Center! Begin today by ordering the Prayer Command Center Kit available from your local Christian bookstore or wherever Christian products are available.

Churches

Pastor Gary V. Whetstone invites you to visit the Victory Christian Fellowship churches, based from one of the fastest-growing churches on the U.S. East Coast. You also can watch live on the Internet. These churches are dedicated to reaching out to meet your family's needs and helping you grow strong spiritually through the revelation knowledge of God's Word. Your faith will be strengthened as you see that Word in action! Visit today or call for prayer:

VICTORY CHRISTIAN FELLOWSHIP IN DELAWARE

100 Wilton Blvd.
New Castle, DE 19720 U.S.A.
Phone: (302) 324-5400
Fax: (302) 324-5448

VICTORY CHRISTIAN FELLOWSHIP IN BALTIMORE, MARYLAND

2929 Sollers Point Rd.
Dundalk, MD 21222-5355
Phone: (410) 282-6201
Fax: (410) 282-6204

Books and the "Life's Answers" Series

Allow the Holy Spirit to educate, liberate, and empower you through Dr. Gary V. Whetstone's books and "Life's Answers" teaching series! Through these studies in God's Word, the Holy Spirit is revealing God's will and purpose to thousands of people. The teachings are full of practical applications to help you achieve your life's goals. Major topics include empowerment, freedom, family and relationships, finances, and prayer. Once you begin this journey of revelation knowledge with Gary Whetstone Worldwide Ministries, you will never be the same again!

Many of these materials are available as books, eBooks, audio cassettes, audio CDs, video CD-ROMs, video cassettes, and VCDs (play on DVD players). To purchase these, contact your local Christian bookstore or other locations where Christian products are available.

School of Biblical Studies

The School of Biblical Studies, a video Bible school Dr. Gary V. Whetstone founded, is a time-proven program that trains champions to live far above ordinary lives. Since 1986, more than twenty thousand students have graduated from this school in more than thirty countries. If you are hungry for all that God has for you, this Bible school will teach you how to obtain it. Whether you take one course or the entire curriculum to pursue your degree, you will walk in greater knowledge of who you are as a child of God and in greater intimacy with Him.

You may choose to study at home through the audio/video Extension School or attend one of the more than 360 Branch School locations worldwide. If you study at home, you may purchase the course materials in your local

Christian bookstore or wherever Christian products are available. The first three classes of the School of Biblical Studies course *Your Liberty in Christ* are available on a free CD-ROM ($60 value) in the back of Gary V. Whetstone's book *Your Liberty in Christ*. Get your copy at your local Christian bookstore or wherever Christian products are available in your area.

Internet Ministry

Our web site at www.gwwm.com is a fountain of spiritual wisdom. Wherever you have access to the web, you have access to our ministry, twenty-four hours a day, seven days a week! There you can find links to send prayer requests; biblical helps; our live TV and radio programs; resources to help answer your questions; our online product catalog of books, eBooks, and audio/video teachings; course descriptions for the School of Biblical Studies; downloads of sample Bible school lessons; ministry information and help; Dr. Gary V. Whetstone's itinerary; and more. Put Gary Whetstone Worldwide Ministries at your fingertips!

ABOUT THE AUTHOR

Gary V. Whetstone is the senior pastor and founder of Victory Christian Fellowship in New Castle, Delaware, and founder of Gary Whetstone Worldwide Ministries. He holds an earned doctorate in Religious Education.

Since personally experiencing God's miraculous deliverance and healing in 1971, Dr. Whetstone has devoted his life to helping others experience freedom through God's Word. Today, he frequently ministers around the world in churches, seminars, and evangelistic crusades. Gifted in teaching, Dr. Whetstone provides practical biblical instruction wherever he ministers and has seen God work powerful signs, wonders, and miracles. Hundreds of thousands have become born-again, Spirit-filled, healed, and set free.

Having a great burden to minister to the local community, Pastor Gary V. Whetstone and his church have launched life-changing outreaches in several areas. These include HIV/AIDS; substance and alcohol abuse; inner-city community outreach centers; Saturday Sidewalk Sunday school; food and clothing outreach programs; and many large evangelistic campaigns, such as the dramatic production "Jesus, Light of the World," which draws over forty-five thousand people annually.

Desiring to spread the truth and good news of the Gospel throughout the world, Dr. Whetstone's passion is to see the Word of God cover the world as the seas cover the earth. This vision is being accomplished through many ministry outreaches. These include sending mission and evangelism teams around the globe; radio and television broadcasting; ministry through the Internet; and the School of Biblical Studies. An extensive audio and video training program, this school equips Christians to experience God's presence and to understand the Bible. Today, this training program is established in hundreds of churches in North and South America, Australia, Europe, Asia, and Africa. In addition to local church and international branch locations, the School of Biblical Studies is available to individuals by extension in their homes using audio cassettes, videotapes, CDs, CD-ROMs, and VCDs. Currently, this home-study program is in English but soon will be available in Spanish and other languages.

Gary V. Whetstone has appeared on many national and international radio and television programs and has authored key books, among which are *The Victorious Walk, How to Identify and Remove Curses!, Make Fear Bow, Millionaire Mentality, Your Liberty in Christ,* and his personal testimony of miraculous deliverance and healing in *Conquering Your Unseen Enemies.* The large number of study guides he has produced are testaments to his gifting in practical biblical teaching and are available for use with his numerous video and audio teaching series. Many of these materials are or soon will be available not only in English, but also in Spanish, French, and other languages.

God has gifted Dr. Whetstone with an incredible business sense and ability, enabling him to publish a series of teachings from *Purchasing and Negotiations* to *Success in Business* and *Millionaire Mentality,* which have aired on his radio and television programs, now called "Life's Answers." These broadcasts currently reach an audience of millions on the East Coast of the United States, in Europe, in Canada, and on the Internet.

Since experiencing God's healing touch himself in 1971, Dr. Gary V. Whetstone has dedicated his life to helping others experience that same healing and freedom in their own lives. As senior pastor and founder of Victory Christian Fellowship in New Castle, Delaware, Dr. Whetstone has organized Inner City Community Outreach Centers, dramatic evangelistic productions, and outreaches to HIV and AIDS victims, among other things.

Dr. Whetstone and his wife of more than thirty years, Faye, have experienced amazing revival in their own marriage and now conduct marriage enrichment seminars for other couples. Dr. Whetstone also conducts many outreaches through missions teams, radio and television broadcasts, Internet ministries, and speaking sessions.